I0208144

MARKETING STRATEGIES FOR THE MATURE MARKET

Marketing Strategies for the Mature Market

George P. Moschis

QUORUM BOOKS

Westport, Connecticut • London

Library of Congress Cataloging-in-Publication Data

Moschis, George P.
    Marketing strategies for the mature market / George P. Moschis.
        p.   cm.
    Includes bibliographical references and index.
    ISBN 0–89930–887–2 (alk. paper)
    1. Marketing—Management.   2. Market segmentation.   3. New
products—Marketing.   4. Aged as consumers.   I. Title.
    HF5415.13.M677   1994
    658.8'02—dc20   94–8542

British Library Cataloguing in Publication Data is available.

Copyright © 1994 by George P. Moschis

All rights reserved. No portion of this book may be
reproduced, by any process or technique, without the
express written consent of the publisher.

Library of Congress Catalog Card Number: 94–8542
ISBN: 0–89930–887–2

First published in 1994

Quorum Books, 88 Post Road West, Westport, CT 06881
An imprint of Greenwood Publishing Group, Inc.

Printed in the United States of America

The paper used in this book complies with the
Permanent Paper Standard issued by the National
Information Standards Organization (Z39.48–1984).

10 9 8 7 6 5 4 3 2 1

HF
5415.13
.M677
1994

JUN 6 1995

In memory of a remarkable man, my father
Parthenios G. Moschis

Contents

PART V. SUMMARY AND RECOMMENDATIONS

Appendixes

Tables and Figure

FIGURE

Acknowledgments

The author would like to thank a number of organizations and individuals who made this book possible. Much of the work reported in this book was sponsored by the American Association of Retired Persons (AARP) Andrus Foundation, and this financial support is gratefully recognized. This project would not have been possible without the input of various organizations that develop and market products and services to older adults. These organizations were instrumental in providing direction and insights into problems and issues around which several areas of this book were developed. Many expert practitioners are also acknowledged for their invaluable suggestions and contributions.

A number of individuals offered valuable help with this book. Dr. Ruth B. Smith, University of Baltimore; Dr. James Kellaris, University of Cincinnati; Dr. Pradeep Korgaonkar, Florida Atlantic University; and Dr. Anil Marthur, Hofstra University, offered invaluable assistance at early stages of this project. Many thanks to several graduate research assistants, especially Olivia Boyce, Euehun Lee, Jill Hull, Munshik Suh, Dong Chul Han, and Kyoung Park, who bore the burden of questionnaire coding, data analysis of the study reported, and manuscript development and proofreading. I thank other students who assisted, namely Laura Maurice, Ann Carlton, Susan Jewell, Bettina May, and Albert Weston. Thanks also to Lynne Feduik Goetz for her editorial assistance.

Further, I deeply thank the participants who completed questionnaires and provided the information included in this book. It is hoped that the information generated will help businesses and government agencies develop strategies and policies that increase their satisfaction and their well-being as consumers in the marketplace.

Finally, I thank my wife, Nancy, for the time she spent proofreading and editing this book.

PART I

OVERVIEW

1

Introduction

The aging population has captured the attention of business, government, and society in general. American businesses are affected by the changing demographics in two important ways. First, they are faced with the reality of a growing consumer segment having unique consumption needs and high discretionary income. Second, the aging population has implications for work force decisions, especially in areas such as job training, employee benefits, and eldercare programs.

In the process of satisfying needs of the aging population, businesses run the risk of crossing the line separating need fulfillment from need creation, which is often associated with high-pressure selling and deceptive practices. Thus, as businesses expand their operations to better serve the older population, government accordingly takes on an increasing responsibility of overseeing business practices and acting as a "watchdog" in the marketplace. Today, one hears of incidents of fraudulent business practices and of actions government takes to protect the older population from them.

Society is also influenced by the maturing population in a number of ways. First, the changing demographics affect families, especially the older persons' relationships with their adult children. With older people living longer and with larger numbers of their children in the work force, there is less time available for adult children (who are the main caregivers to older family members) to provide their parents with the desired or necessary support with day-to-day activities.

Given these demographic trends and their effects on business, government, and society, consumer researchers and scientists in general have increasingly become interested in understanding the aging population.

Much of the available knowledge is in the form of anecdotal evidence, and many large-scale studies provide inconclusive data about the mature market (Moschis 1992b). Consumer researchers have generated data on older people's consumer behavior, but they have little background in social sciences (especially gerontology) to be in a position to provide explanations for such behaviors that would help practitioners. Social scientists, on the other hand, work in nonbusiness fields; they have the background to better understand human behavior in late life but have little incentive or training to translate such general information into recommendations for business action.

FOCUS OF THE BOOK

Given the increasing interest in the maturing marketplace, the present state of knowledge about marketing to older consumers, and the existing knowledge dispersed in nonbusiness fields that can be potentially useful in understanding older consumers, this book has several objectives:

1. It summarizes the existing knowledge about the behavior of older adults as consumers.
2. It provides background information useful in helping practitioners understand reasons for consumer behavior in late life.
3. By presenting new evidence from a large-scale study, the book supplements and expands knowledge on how to market to the aging population.
4. On the basis of the evidence presented, the book draws conclusions and recommends courses of action to business practitioners interested in better serving the older consumer market.

The main purpose of this book is to organize and present information useful in developing strategies for tapping the increasingly important mature consumer market. Using the strategic marketing process as a framework, the information is organized as it may apply to specific stages in the strategic marketing process. Thus, the book begins with information relevant to the analysis of the mature market, such as size and wealth, and how this market differs from other consumer markets. Next, it presents information useful in analyzing opportunities that exist within this market in the form of unfilled needs, as well as information related to segmentation and market targeting. An analysis of market behavior is presented next, focusing on financial and consumption lifestyles as well as the information needs of older consumers. Next, older consumers' orientations toward business offerings and strategies are analyzed, focusing on responses in all the areas of the marketing mix (i.e., new product development, pricing, distribution, promotion) and drawing implications for specific courses of business action. Finally, an effort is made to summarize the information using a strategic marketing framework, making recommendations on how to market to this segment of the population.

By presenting information within the context of specific strategic marketing decisions, the book focuses on assisting marketers in answering questions relevant to specific stages of strategy development. Information related to each specific marketing decision stage comes from two main sources: published studies and a large-scale national study by the author. The latter is used to fill gaps in existing knowledge and assists in recommending specific strategies for marketing to the mature market.

In order to help the reader relate information to relevant areas of the strategic marketing process, a brief overview of the main strategic concepts follows.

AN OVERVIEW OF THE STRATEGIC MARKETING PROCESS

The strategic marketing management process includes analysis of business growth opportunities, market segmentation and targeting or positioning, and development of marketing programs.

Types of Growth Opportunities

Opportunities for growth can be labeled as intensive, integrative, and diversification (Kotler 1984).

Intensive Growth

Intensive growth opportunities refer to those available to a business in its current operations. Such opportunities are attractive to companies that have not fully exploited opportunities associated with their current products and markets. Intensive growth opportunities include *market penetration, market development,* and *product development.*

Market penetration refers to a company's growth by selling its current products to its current markets through more aggressive marketing efforts. For example, a firm can get its current customers to buy a larger number of its products and services (i.e., product lines) or to replace products faster, it can attract competitors' customers, or it can induce nonusers in its current market areas to start using its products. The fact that mature consumers are generally light users of many products and services (Moschis 1992b) presents an opportunity for market penetration. For example, product use can be increased by offering incentives to buy them (e.g., price discounts) and by making products more functionally suitable to the elderly who are physically impaired. Other examples of better marketing of existing products include the development of advertising appeals and sales promotion strategies that would stimulate greater demand.

Market development refers to a company's growth by selling its current products to new markets. A company can expand geographically by selling its products in new geographic territories. It can also attempt to sell its products to more diversified types of customers or consumer segments of the market. The fact that the mature market has been ignored (Moschis 1992b) presents an opportunity for market development. The decision to go international is also an example of this type of expansion. Market development is warranted as a viable strategy when present markets are saturated and keen competition exists.

Finally, *product development* refers to a company's growth by developing and selling new or improved products for its existing markets. For example, a company can develop new models and sizes, it can create different product-quality versions, and it can modify existing products to better serve older customer needs.

Integrative Growth

Integrative growth is desirable for firms in industries that have growth potential and in situations where a company can increase its profitability, control, or overall efficiency by integrating with other companies at the same or different levels of distribution in the same industry. A company may seek *backward*, *forward*, or *horizontal integration*.

Backward integration refers to a firm's acquisition or ownership of, or increased control over, its supply system. This appears to be an attractive growth opportunity when suppliers enjoy high growth and profitability or when there is uncertainty about the availability of supplies. For example, backward-integration opportunities for a telecommunications company would be the acquisition of manufacturers of computers and other telecommunications equipment/components the company presently purchases from its suppliers.

Forward integration refers to a firm's acquisition of ownership or increased control over its distribution system. While high growth or profitability of distributors is often a reason for forward integration, other factors such as need for greater control over point-of-sale and after-sale service often serve as reasons. Companies often achieve forward integration by marketing their products directly to the consumer (e.g., mail order, telemarketing).

Horizontal integration entails a company's growth by acquisition or increase in control over its competitors. Small, fast-growing firms are often attractive targets for takeovers, effectively providing the larger companies with new talent. For example, industry observers consider Apple as a candidate for acquisition by one of the data-processing giants not currently in the personal computer field.

Diversification

One type of growth opportunity—diversification—usually exists outside the sphere of production and marketing activities or capabilities. Three types of diversification growth opportunities can be distinguished: *concentric, horizontal,* and *conglomerate.*

Concentric diversification refers to a company's growth opportunities through adding new products having technological and marketing synergies with its existing product lines; these new products are most likely to appeal to new classes of customers. For example, health monitoring/diagnostic equipment and emergency alarm systems have synergies with existing technologies (equipment and network), yet they are likely to appeal to a smaller segment—that is, older and perhaps upscale customers. Another example of this type of diversification is Bell Atlantic Corporation's recent announcement to team with a small New Jersey company to provide 60 channels of television over new high-capacity lines to 38,000 homes in Dover Township, New Jersey. Telephone companies are barred by federal law from owning cable television systems in the market in which they provide telephone services.

Horizontal diversification refers to a company's growth opportunities via development of products that are unrelated to existing products but that could appeal to its current customers. Examples of this type of diversification are General Motors (GM) and AT&T's decisions to market financial services.

Conglomerate diversification refers to a firm's effort to grow by adding new products for new classes of customers; the new products have no relationship to existing products or classes of customers. The reason for conglomerate diversification can be a desire to offset some deficiency or to take advantage of some business opportunity. This growth opportunity is likely to involve the greatest risks. An example of conglomerate diversification is the Minneapolis-based First Bank System, Inc., which recently decided to offer bank-at-home services and to serve as a clearinghouse for push-button retail purchases for several retailers; its market includes agribusinesses. The possible development of the home or office of the future would require the synergy of several types of industries, including builders, hardware, and telecommunications companies.

Market Segmentation and Targeting

The next step in the strategic marketing management process involves segmenting the market and selecting target markets. This step is necessary before developing marketing strategies (Kotler 1984).

Market Segmentation

Market segmentation involves breaking down the entire market into smaller submarkets or subgroups that can be reached more effectively with different marketing programs. The question of market segmentation is a managerial one—that is, *should* the market be segmented? That is, are the *statistically significant* differences found among segments (for example, age groups) also *managerially significant*? To answer the second question, one must examine the benefits of market segmentation vis-à-vis its costs. To make this type of assessment, one must first determine whether any statistically significant differences between, for example, two segments justify the cost of developing target marketing (target marketing distinguishes among many market segments, selects one or more of these segments, and develops products and marketing mixes tailored to each segment). For instance, consider a 10 percent difference among younger and older customers desiring a particular telecommunication service. If one wishes to consider different marketing strategies to appeal to these two segments, one should examine whether a 10 percent difference in service desirability between the two segments justifies the extra cost associated with the development of two strategies rather than one. Ideally, the 10 percent should be translated into numbers of customers and potential revenues. Potential revenues could be estimated by calculating the proportion of those expressing intentions to use ("definitely/probably would use") and those who are expected to use it and continue using it (retention rate). Furthermore, a more precise estimate of the importance of each segment in terms of potential revenues must include not only the number of potential users but also the monthly or usage rate (in the latter case "frequency of use" or "rate" should be used). The costs associated with target marketing may include the cost of developing an entirely different marketing mix for each segment. To the extent that segments differ in the way they respond to the seller's efforts, different marketing efforts aimed at each segment are needed and often justified.

Market Coverage Strategies

If differences among segments of a market are small or do not justify developing different strategies for each, a firm may choose to ignore market segment differences and go after the whole market with the same marketing program. In doing so, the emphasis should be placed upon identifying the commonalities rather than differences among needs of consumers in different segments. This approach keeps down marketing costs but relies on mass distribution and mass advertising aimed primarily at the largest segment of the market. Alternately, the company may decide to appeal to several segments by developing separate offers for each. This "differentiated" marketing strategy usually creates more total sales than an undifferentiated strategy and also increases the cost of doing business, especially production and promotion costs. There is always a third possibility—concentrate on one or just a few subsegments. This strategy allows the company to achieve operating economies because of specialization.

Each strategy appears to be desirable under different conditions.

- *Differentiated marketing* is preferred when products/services sold are capable of feature variations such as telecommunication services/products, when the product or service has been in existence for a long time and faces strong competition, and when the market has different needs, tastes, and reacts differently to marketing appeals.
- *Undifferentiated marketing* should be used when the company's product is homogeneous (like commodities), when buyers have the same tastes and react the same way to marketing appeals, and when the firm introduces a new product of potentially wide appeal and acceptance.
- *Concentrated marketing* is suggested when a firm's resources are limited, when products/services can be subject to variations in features, and when the firm introduces a new product likely to be of interest to a select group of customers.

The three strategies should also be evaluated in the context of competitor's practices. For example, when competitors practice undifferentiated marketing, much can be gained by pursuing differentiated or concentrated marketing strategy (Kotler 1984). When a company tries to appeal to select groups of customers who have unique needs that are not effectively served by competitors, it usually uses a differentiated strategy aimed at developing a "niche" in the market. When a company tries to set itself apart from its competitors by appealing to the needs of selected groups of customers, the company attempts to *position* itself or its products.

Developing Marketing Programs

After choosing target markets, marketing programs or plans for action must be designed to reach these markets. This process involves tactical strategic decisions on specific marketing activities, including decisions on levels of marketing expenditures and dozens of elements of the marketing mix such as pricing, distribution, and promotion decisions. Examples of pricing strategies include decisions on whether the product should be priced at competitive levels, a skimming strategy should be used where high introductory prices are set, or the company should use penetration pricing, where the company sets a relatively low price in an effort to quickly penetrate the market. Examples of distribution strategies involve decisions on the types and numbers of distribution outlets that should provide incentives to distributors to promote the product ("push" strategy) or to create consumer demand ("pull" strategy). Examples of promotion decisions include decisions on the types of promotion that should be used (e.g., advertising and sales promotions) as well as decisions on specific promotional strategies such as media and message strategies. Finally, a sound marketing plan should include guidelines for measuring the effectiveness of the firm's marketing activities and should spell out ways for evaluating how well the overall strategy is being implemented.

ORGANIZATION OF THE BOOK

The approach used to accomplish the purpose and objectives of this book focuses on providing relevant information on questions that marketing strategists must answer in order to better market to the aging population. Specifically, the book identifies key issues of interest to marketing strategists, and then organizes and presents information useful in answering or resolving these issues. This approach is used because it parallels the thinking of businesses that contemplate marketing to the older population. Key issues addressed include:

- Is the mature market a viable market?
- Should the older consumer market be considered as a separate or unique market, or should it be regarded as a part of the entire consumer market?
- Should the mature market be treated as a homogeneous market, or should it be segmented?
- What motivates consumer behavior in late life, especially with respect to buying products? How could companies use older consumer needs and motives to develop new products and services? How should they position such products?
- If segmentation is needed, what is the best way to segment the mature market?
- How do older people use their financial resources, and how do such money-management practices and financial lifestyles affect consumption?
- What sources of information do older people rely on in making purchasing decisions? How can businesses better promote to older consumers, or inform them about, their products and services?
- How do older people respond to new products, especially technological innovations designed to enhance their well-being?
- What are older persons' opinions on existing products and services? How satisfied are they? What changes in the existing products should be made?
- How do older people respond to various promotional practices?
- How do mature adults respond to age-targeted marketing practices?
- What do mature consumers think of existing distribution outlets and distribution modes? How can businesses effectively distribute products and services to them?

While the book addresses such broad issues, attention is also given to specific subissues of interest to business strategists. For example, for broad areas such as age-based marketing strategies, the book presents information useful in addressing the effectiveness of specific strategies (e.g., use of older models in ads, products for older people, senior discounts). Similarly, the effectiveness of consumer information sources is analyzed in the context of specific media for specific types of products.

This book has twelve chapters. After this "Introduction," which presents a brief overview of the strategic marketing management process, the first three issues listed above are addressed in Chapter 2, with each of the remaining nine issues addressed in each of the chapters that follow, respectively. The final chapter summarizes key findings, draws conclusions, and makes recommendations to marketing decision makers; it also highlights major findings within the strategic marketing management framework. In addressing the various issues, data from a national survey are used extensively along with information from previous research studies. Thus, rather than relying on anecdotal evidence, this book provides decision makers with information based on empirical evidence. Whenever feasible the research findings are interpreted in the context of strategic marketing decisions to help practitioners design strategies to effectively serve the aging population.

2

The Mature Consumer Market

Before we can begin discussing the mature consumer market, a definition of this market is needed. Generally speaking, when we think of the mature market we think of an older group of people. However, there is considerable debate over the minimum age cutoff that defines this market and differentiates it from the younger population. Recent reviews of studies in academia and industry (Moschis 1992b) show that the minimum age for this market ranges between 45 and 65. This should not come as a surprise because it is often the product or service targeted at this market that defines its age composition. For example, the mature consumer market for travel and entertainment is expected to be different, usually much younger, than the market for nursing homes. Thus, there are stereotypes as to the age composition of the mature market.

For the purpose of discussion here, we adapt a compromising view of the age composition of the mature market. The mature market refers to individuals age 55 and older. Using this definition, the size of this market was estimated at 53 million in 1991, according to the U.S. Bureau of the Census. The large majority of this group consists of people between the ages of 55 and 64 (22 million or 41%), with another 18 million (34%) between the ages of 65 and 74. Thus, this segment of the population is skewed to the younger age side. However, the market's age distribution is expected to change as the 76 million baby boomers begin to swell the ranks of the mature consumer market at the turn of the century. In approximately fifty years, there will be an even age distribution of older Americans across the three main age brackets (55–64, 65–74, 75+), and its total size is expected to double (Moschis 1992b). The very old group (85+) will continue to outpace the growth of other population segments; it is currently growing six times faster than the rest of the population.

What do these numbers mean in terms of market size and market potential for goods and services? In order to answer this question, one must examine these numbers in concert with ability to spend. First, the 55+ market, presently constituting 21 percent of the U.S. population, will gradually increase to 33 percent during the next fifty years. This will mostly likely force many marketers to think differently about their target markets. The focus is likely to shift from "youth orientation," placing a greater emphasis on the older consumer. This shift is likely to be facilitated by the increasing wealth in the hands of older Americans.

FINANCIAL WEALTH

The prevailing view regarding the financial well-being of older people is rather negative. This stereotype was developed (and still tends to persist) to a larger extent prior to the second half of this century. The economic conditions of older Americans, however, have drastically changed in recent years. Social Security benefits have helped place nearly half of the recipients above the poverty line, while several corporate and retirement benefits have boosted their incomes and financial status. Today, more households than ever before have working spouses whose incomes, government benefits, and retirement benefits contribute to the household's economic power. Finally, much of the older person's economic well-being is supported by what we refer to as "imputed benefits." These benefits are in the form of tax "breaks" such as federal income tax and Social Security exemptions, and cash benefits from Medicare insurance programs.

Income, of course, is often the single most common criterion used in determining a person's financial well-being. *Household income* tends to be highest right before retirement, usually between the ages of 55 and 65. After age 65, people in a household are likely to be retired, and the household size gets smaller. Thus, household income in late life may not be an accurate criterion of the older person's economic well-being, and *per capita income* might be a more accurate predictor of how well an older person does financially. When the latter criterion is used, older persons fare much better than most younger adults. However, per capita income does not factor in the many imputed benefits available to older people, and *discretionary income* is considered to be an even more accurate predictor of the older person's economic power and spending ability. This criterion considers the amount of money available to the older person, after excluding expenses needed to maintain a comfortable standard of living. This is an important indicator of the mature market's buying power because it measures ability to spend on nonessential items such as luxury products and vacations. Based on this criterion, people 55 and over fare rather well.

People age 55 and over, although they make up only 22 percent of the population, have more than half of this country's discretionary income. It is also interesting to note that people age 65 and over have the highest per capita discretionary income. However, having money does not mean spending it. Most older people hold on to a sizeable portion of their incomes for several reasons. First, they do not have as many consumption needs as they used to have earlier in life. For example, leaving the labor force might decrease the need for spending on clothing and cosmetics. Second, older consumers are aware of the high costs of health care and long-term care and the need to save in the event of illness or long-term institutionalization. There may also be some negative attitudes toward spending instilled in older people who experienced the Great Depression. Researchers at the University of Pennsylvania, after extensive analysis of data collected by the U.S. Department of Labor between 1960 and 1986, concluded that the elderly are more likely to save than to spend, while baby boomers are engaged in a virtual consumption binge into their middle age (Moschis 1992b). While these findings might suggest the influence of Great Depression experiences, some of these differences might be due to the fact that younger people have a longer time horizon to accumulate wealth and plan for retirement. The fact that older people save suggests that they have sizeable net worth. Indeed, the conference board estimated that people age 55 and older control more than three-fourths of this country's assets (Moschis 1992b). As Table 2.1 shows, older consumers have sizeable assets of various types.

While older adults tend to save more than younger Americans, this does not mean that they do not spend or spend less than their younger counterparts. Rather, people age 55 and over spend more per household as well as on a per capita basis. However, older adults show a relatively greater propensity to save than to spend.

EXPENDITURE PATTERNS

Older people vary a great deal in the way they spend their money. Factors such as family size, income, age, and sex are likely to influence the older person's consumption patterns. According to the U.S. Bureau of Labor Statistics' *Consumer Expenditure Survey* (1989), households headed by individuals age 55 and over spent more than $729 billion on goods and services in 1989, or 27.36 percent of the total spending by all U.S. households. On a per capita basis, the average older person spent nearly $14,000 annually, in comparison with $10,600 for the average person in this country. Table 2.2 shows expenditures in various categories by age group of older persons. The table also shows the total expenditures of all household units as well as the amount and percentage of the total spent by households headed by older adults. These percentage figures do not take into account the size of the household. However, it can be concluded that expenditures vary greatly by age group and type of expenditure category.

Table 2.1
Average Value of Holdings for Asset Owners by Age of Householder

	All Households	55 – 64	65 and over Total	65–69	70–74	75+
Mean Value of Holdings of Assets	92,017	147,679	136,013	149,495	155,795	112,645
Interest–earning assets at financial institutions (1)	17,823	23,706	38,505	34,050	43,543	38,743
Other interest–earning assets (2)	40,786	44,732	65,973	75,887	68,920	54,951
Regular checking accounts	1,054	1,423	1,436	1,375	1,649	1,332
Stocks and mutual funds	27,373	37,552	49,493	36,881	84,889	36,601
Equity in business or profession	64,534	87,045	74,154	69,829	75,694	82,532
Equity in motor vehicles	6,205	7,725	5,714	6,595	6,104	4,424
Equity in own home	62,246	77,214	73,587	79,295	77,237	67,316
Rental property equity	80,350	98,530	81,175	88,441	78,300	75,967
Other real estate equity	37,523	43,919	35,688	37,487	31,850	37,286
U.S. savings bonds	2,963	5,289	7,206	66,423	8,728	6,979
IRA or KEOGH accounts	16,062	22,304	25,486	27,152	27,756	12,535
Other assets (3)	41,309	47,937	57,351	49,033	60,701	62,569

---

(1) Includes passbook savings accounts, money market deposit accounts, CDs, and interest-earning
   checking accounts.
(2) Includes money market funds, U.S. Government securities, municipal and corporate bonds, and
   other interest-earning assets.
(3) Includes mortgages held from sale of real estate, amount due from sale of a business, unit trusts,
   and other financial investments.

Source: U.S. Bureau of the Census (1990).

Certain categories such as health care and cash contributions clearly stand
out as major categories of income outlay. For other categories the magnitude of spending among older adults is not as obvious. However, by
considering these statistics on a per capita basis, additional information
can be obtained.

On a per capita basis, older households spend on food about 10 percent
more than the national average. Average spending at restaurants is higher
but declines after age 75. Consumption of alcoholic beverages declines
sharply with age. Spending on housing by older Americans is lower than
the national average, since most older households have paid off their mortgages. Despite this, however, older Americans spend as much per capita
on housing as younger adults as a result of smaller size of households and
increasing maintenance (repair/remodeling) expenses due to the aging of
the house. Expenditures on clothing also decline in late life as the older
person tends to withdraw from settings that demand greater attention to
apparel, as in the case of employment at an office.

The major expense item that drastically increases with age is health care.
About half of this country's expenditures on health care are incurred by

Table 2.2
Annual Expenditures and Characteristics of All Consumer Units by Age of Reference Person

Item	All Consumer Units	55 - 64	65 - 74	75 and over	Total 55 and over	% Of Total
Number of consumer units ('000s)	95,818	12,005	11,848	8,474	32,327	33.74%
Annual expenditures ($'000,000s)	$2,664,699	$343,547	$250,609	$134,898	$729,054	27.36
Food	397,836	53,110	37,973	21,227	112,310	28.23
Food at home	229,005	31,345	24,265	14,516	70,126	30.62
Cereals and bakery products	34,399	4,610	3,614	2,534	10,757	31.27
Meats, poultry, fish, and eggs	58,545	8,512	6,339	3,449	18,299	31.26
Dairy products	29,129	3,782	2,891	1,881	8,554	29.37
Fruits and vegetables	39,094	5,462	4,858	3,025	13,345	34.14
Other food at home	67,839	8,992	6,552	3,627	19,171	28.26
Food away from home	168,831	21,765	13,708	6,711	42,185	24.99
Alcoholic beverages	27,212	3,277	2,014	763	6,054	22.25
Housing	824,897	97,973	80,247	45,116	223,335	27.07
Shelter	463,280	51,862	38,897	21,812	112,571	24.30
Owned dwellings	273,081	35,043	23,779	11,321	70,143	25.69
Rented dwellings	143,727	8,860	10,331	8,245	27,436	19.09
Other lodging	46,472	7,959	4,798	2,246	15,003	32.28
Utilities, fuels, and public services	175,826	24,286	21,480	12,948	58,715	33.39
Household operations	44,076	4,166	4,384	3,991	12,541	28.45
Housekeeping supplies	37,752	4,970	4,597	2,678	12,245	32.43
Household furnishings and equipment	104,058	12,689	10,888	3,678	27,255	26.19
Apparel and services	151,584	18,956	13,483	4,881	37,320	24.62
Transportation	497,008	64,239	43,778	19,050	127,067	25.57
Vehicle purchases (net outlay)	219,519	27,467	17,109	8,771	53,347	24.30
Gasoline and motor oil	94,381	13,013	8,933	3,178	25,125	26.62
Other vehicle expenses	155,896	19,832	14,170	5,584	39,587	25.39
Public transportation	27,212	3,938	3,566	1,517	9,021	33.15
Health care	134,816	21,777	23,471	19,922	65,170	48.34
Entertainment	136,445	16,459	9,988	4,627	31,074	22.77
Personal care products and services	35,069	4,862	3,720	1,907	10,489	29.91
Reading	15,043	2,089	1,872	932	4,893	32.53
Education	35,165	3,073	1,137	280	4,490	12.77
Tobacco products and smoking supplies	25,008	3,878	2,227	754	6,859	27.43
Miscellaneous	61,611	7,971	6,042	2,890	16,903	27.44
Cash contributions	86,236	13,794	12,109	10,059	35,961	41.70
Personal insurance and pensions	236,862	32,089	12,547	2,500	47,136	19.90
Life and other personal insurance	33,153	4,706	4,289	1,542	10,537	31.78
Pensions and Social Security	203,613	27,383	8,258	958	36,599	17.97

Source: U.S. Bureau of Labor Statistics (1989).

households headed by adults age 55 and older. On a per capita basis, of course, this expenditure is much higher. Another major outlay is cash contributions. Older people give a lot more to charities than younger adults, both in terms of absolute dollars as well as in proportion to their income. In addition, they spend a large sum of money on gifts for relatives.

Expenditures on other discretionary items such as travel and entertainment vary by select characteristics of the older person. For example, expenditures on travel are very high among upscale older people. Similarly, expenditures on financial services, transportation, and housing (vacation homes) sharply increase with increasing income in late life.

A UNIQUE MARKET

The mature consumer market is a unique market. It is comprised of older Americans who differ from younger people. Furthermore, mature adults composing this market are likely to differ from those who made up the mature markets of the past. Three major reasons are responsible for the uniqueness of this market.

First, older people are at a different stage of biophysical and psychosocial maturation than younger adults. They have different needs resulting from the aging of body systems and the onset of disease (e.g., arthritis), such as a need for certain dietary products and easy-to-open jars or packages. Similarly, older adults have aged psychologically, and this is likely to reflect in their ability to reason, remember, and solve problems. They differ from younger people with respect to their perceptions of themselves as older people (self-concept) and their personality—that is, how others see them. Finally, older adults are likely to have aged socially in that they may accept or enact roles subscribed to them by society such as the role of "retiree," "grandparent," or "old person." Thus, older people are at a different stage of biophysical, psychological, and social maturation and, as a result, are likely to behave differently than their younger counterparts who have yet to face these circumstances in life.

A second reason why the mature market is unique is because the people included in it have accumulated different types of experiences over the longer period than their younger counterparts. Such experiences tend to affect their consumer behavior, including the meaning they attach to various products and the criteria they use in purchasing them. Consumption has different meanings based on one's stage in life. For example, to a younger person a house may be viewed as an investment or even a status symbol, while to an older person, living in a house could be viewed as a means of maintaining one's independence and self-esteem. Such differences in experiences and perceptions between younger and older persons make the mature market a unique market.

The final reason for differentiating this segment from younger age segments of the consumer market is that people who compose it have experienced similar sets of circumstances that differ from those experienced by younger people. For example, most mature Americans, especially those age 65 and over, experienced the Great Depression, which may have affected their consumer behavior, in comparison to their younger counterparts who grew up during more prosperous times. Most baby boomers were brought up in front of a television set. By the time the average baby boomer reaches the age of 65, he or she will have spent an average of eleven years in front of the TV, something which is not the case among today's elderly. And today's children and teenagers who use personal computers in school or at home will have different attitudes toward technologies when they reach the ranks of the mature market in comparison to today's adults. Thus, different cohorts experience different sets of circumstances in their lives that are likely to affect their behavior in the marketplace, making today's mature market unique.

A HETEROGENEOUS MARKET

Although the mature market is a unique market, it is by no means a homogeneous one. This is a common mistake marketers often make by assuming that older people are all alike, lumping them into one category and treating them the same in their marketing efforts. Reality is that the mature market is a highly diversified market, regardless of the criteria one uses to define heterogeneity, whether these are demographic factors; health, psychological, or social criteria; or lifestyle characteristics. Older Americans markedly differ amongst themselves along any dimension used to define them or describe them as a segment.

With respect to age, older Americans are not uniformly distributed along the various age brackets, with differences in age distribution likely to be affected by birth and life expectancy rates. Sex composition also differs on the basis of age, with women outnumbering men by two to one at age 75. While they appear to have high incomes, half of Americans age 65 and over actually fall below the poverty level in the absence of Social Security benefits, suggesting a highly skewed distribution of income among people of this market. With respect to other demographic characteristics such as living arrangements, geographic location, and education, the mature market shows a much higher variability in comparison to the variability observed in the rest of the population (Moschis 1992b).

Turning to criteria such as health and biophysical factors in general, one can observe a wide variability among the aged population. People not only age differently but also at different rates. The phrase "you don't look your age" is more commonly applied to older than to younger people. Similarly, not every disease associated with old age is common to all people of a certain age. Simply, some people are healthier than others at a certain age, and differences in health and ability to function reflect upon the older person's consumption activities.

Finally, older people differ psychologically, socially, and even spiritually. Some people are mentally alert into their 80s and 90s, while others become cognitively impaired at a much younger age. Their personalities and attitudes are also likely to become more intensified and diverse rather than become uniform with age. Some people accept older age, while others reject it and are of the opinion that they still feel and act younger than their chronological age. Finally, people age socially at markedly different rates. Some withdraw from social activities and join groups of other disengaged people (e.g., senior citizen centers), while others maintain active lifestyles, doing the things they have been doing all their life. In short, some people "act their age" while others don't. These differences in psychological state of mind and social lifestyle are likely to result in differences in consumer behavior in the marketplace since consumer behavior is influenced by psychological and social factors.

In sum, the mature market is a viable and growing market. It differs from markets comprised of younger age groups because of a number of experiential, biophysical, and psychosocial factors. These and other factors are also responsible for the wide heterogeneity in the older population and can affect consumer behavior. Thus, it becomes necessary for marketers to carefully examine and analyze the mature market before developing market strategies.

PART II

IDENTIFYING OPPORTUNITIES

3

Analyzing Needs of Older Adults

Changes in the older person's biophysical and psychosocial states tend to be manifested in behavioral and cognitive changes. Such changes can be in the form of needs, attitudes, values, abilities or skills, and behaviors. By understanding the dynamics characterizing the aging process, one might be able to understand these types of changes in attitudes and behaviors of older adults, as well as their resultant needs. This chapter lays the foundation for understanding the rationale for studying older consumer behavior from the perspective of need development. These needs can be used as a focal point for developing new products and marketing strategies; this chapter offers such an illustration.

While many needs of older adults are very similar to those of their younger counterparts, most older adults are likely to exhibit needs that differ from those they experienced at earlier stages in life. This is because aging is associated with changes within the person as well as in the person's environment. To better understand how needs develop as a result of these changes, one must examine specific processes of aging and the effects of those processes on need development.

Aging is a complex and multidimensional process. People age as biological beings, psychological beings, and social beings. Biological aging refers to the changes in cells and tissues resulting in the physical deterioration of the biological system and its susceptibility to disease and mortality. Psychological aging involves changes in mental functioning, personality, and self-perception. Finally, social aging refers to the changing composite of social lifestyles, attributes, attitudes, and an assumption of social roles people are expected to play at various stages in life (e.g., "parent," "retiree," "grandparent").

As people grow older they are likely to experience major economic adjustments due to retirement. They may also face emotional traumas due to illness or loss of a spouse and lifelong friends. We call such disturbances "risk points," which can affect the older person's sense of well-being, interactions with other people, and even self-confidence. In late life people tend to be concerned with their health care and their financial security. They are reluctant to give up their independence, and they do not want to be a burden to anyone.

There are relatively few psychological changes that occur with age. Many older people have the same feelings they had when they were younger. For example, they keep their sense of humor and they want romance to continue to be part of their life. However, because this society has become "youth oriented," older people in the United States are not always looked upon with respect. As people grow older they become increasingly sensitive to aging, and they are very sensitive to the way younger people respond to them.

In order to serve the older consumer effectively, marketers must be aware that older people want to be treated as any person wants to be treated—with dignity and respect. However, because of the aging process, chances are that there will be changes in needs and attitudes natural to the aging process. These changes develop due to psychological, social, or physiological changes that can occur with aging.

While one does not have to be old to experience physiological changes, many such changes are more likely to occur in late life. As we age there are some changes that affect our vision. At age 50, for example, normal eyes admit half the light that the eyes of a person in his or her 20s do. This makes it harder for older persons to read smaller print, especially in poor light or when there is glare. They may also have difficulty detecting differences in color. Vision can be affected by disease (e.g., cataracts, glaucoma, diabetes) as well. Another change that gradually occurs with age is hearing loss, especially among people who have been exposed to frequent loud noise earlier in life. As people get older they may lose the ability to hear certain frequencies of sound, especially high-pitched sounds; other sounds tend to blend together. As a result, older people prefer when others speak slowly, clearly, and with good diction. Being hard of hearing may make older people appear stupid, which hurts their self-esteem and pride. Also, with age, people begin to experience changes in dexterity. Many older people have arthritis, which makes it difficult for them to write or open a jar.

Certain emotional changes or risk points can have a tremendous impact on a person's state of mind. For example, death of a spouse can cause deep depression, which affects the person's psychological and social well-being.

Because of these physiological and psychosocial changes, older people are likely to need special attention and require an understanding of their perceptions and concerns. Thus, it is important for marketers to understand these needs and concerns in order to better respond to them.

NATURE OF NEEDS

One major consequence of changes occurring in the aging person is the development of new needs or the change in existing ones. *Need* is a multifaceted, multidimensional concept and, thus, not easy to define. Virginia C. Little (1980, p. 65) summarizes the problems of assessing the needs of the aged: "National and international efforts to assess the needs of the elderly confront common problems: lack of an accepted definition of terms such as 'need,' 'want' and 'demand;' perceptions vary with age, professional role, relationship and time; a range of methodologies encompassing rational, empirical and relativistic approaches, as well as subjective, objective and statistical measures."

To illustrate the freedom one has in working with needs, one study defined needs in terms of problems, services, and community support; they were uniformly measured across life domains such as employment, environment, and social domain (Murrell, Brockway, and Schulte 1982). Furthermore, measurement of needs can take place at different levels, from broad (e.g., need for adequate health care services) to specific (need for physiotherapy). The sections that follow summarize needs of older adults expressed or identified as "concerns," "problems," "fears," and "interests."

Concerns

The types of concerns the aged population expressed in several studies vary widely and are not consistent across studies. Furthermore, the types of concerns expressed by older adults tend to vary by background characteristics.

John R. Burton and Charles B. Hennon (1980) asked urban and rural residents in three age groups (55–64, 65–74, 75+) to indicate their level of concern in thirty-two consumer areas. The following ranking of these concerns was obtained, although they may not be representative of the U.S. population because those surveyed came from senior centers:

Utilities	50.16%
Food	47.02%
Clothing	34.06%
Home repairs	33.44%

Taxes	32.40%
Auto	31.68%
Health and hospital insurance	31.15%
Medical services	30.84%
Prescription drugs	29.60%
Eye care	28.57%
Auto insurance	28.04%
Home security	27.73%

A Yankelovich study conducted for the Markle Foundation (1988) not only assessed levels of concern among older adults but also differences in such levels by age among adults 45 years of age and older. People did not show significant differences across age groups in the level of concern. In relation to the younger group (45–59), those 60 and over were found to be relatively content and secure. It is not until the age of 80 when people feel significantly less secure.

Another study conducted by the Roper Organization found eight out of ten of those over 45 to be very concerned with crime and loneliness (Ziff 1984). However, it is not clear that these concerns are unique only to the older population. In the Doyle Dane Bernbach (DDB) Trend Study (Ziff 1984), more than four out of ten older adults indicated substantial levels of concern with the possibility of being neglected by family and friends, being lonely, and being farther away from home. Again, no information about the level of concern with these happenings was reported for younger age groups.

In an American Association of Retired Persons (AARP) (1986) study of a national sample of 1,500 persons age 60 and over, a number of specific concerns were investigated, many related to housing and living conditions. AARP found that this group of older Americans are concerned with their possessions, health, and social relations. Although no information was given comparing these responses to younger age groups, information was revealed on how these responses differ by specific age subgroup. Age differences in concerns expressed are not uniform across demographic characteristics. For example, there are sex differences in expressed concerns. Men are more concerned about having to take care of a loved one than women (48.0% versus 40.0%); men over age 80 are more concerned with having to live with someone if they don't want to than women over 80 (47.0% versus 36.0%); and men are more concerned than women about leaving something for their families after they are gone (34.0% versus 25.0%).

Table 3.1
Consumption-Related Needs and Concerns of Younger (under 55) and Older (55+) Adults (percentage "concerned a lot")

	Younger	Older
Money		
Being able to keep up with bills and weekly expenses	49.93	30.21
Being financially independent	55.66	46.01
Health/Well-Being		
Being able to contact someone in case of emergency	41.48	27.92
Being able to take care of yourself physically when you get older	39.13	52.77
Social/Family		
Having to take care of your aging parents	21.97	11.93
Feeling that no one cares for you	13.12	7.99
Home		
Having your home/apartment burned or burglarized	40.84	41.27
Finding someone to do home or appliance repairs	15.74	22.43
Information		
Getting useful information on things that affect you	49.90	37.78
Getting good financial, tax, or legal advice	44.91	35.02
Leisure		
Finding ways to enjoy yourself (like travel and entertainment)	30.55	19.67
Being able to attend special events or activities	16.67	10.83
Daily Activities		
Being able to do your shopping and run errands	26.02	27.44
Being able to fix your meals	21.48	20.19

Although the AARP study did not compare concerns between younger and older adults, an unpublished study conducted by the author for the Center for Mature Consumer Studies (CMCS) provides information on how older adults (55+) differ from their younger counterparts. Specifically, older respondents are more likely to be concerned with crime, finding someone to do home or appliance repairs, and knowing where to call for assistance on what to do or how to do certain things. Younger adults, on the other hand, express a greater concern in areas such as finances, leisure activities, and social relations. Table 3.1 shows responses to these topics given by the 55-and-over sample, as well as by the younger respondents. Money-related issues are of main concern among older adults. Forty-six percent say they are "concerned a lot" with being financially independent. Similarly, a little over 30 percent are concerned with keeping up with bills and weekly expenses in general. Despite concerns with money, older adults appear to be financially well-off in comparison to their younger counterparts. More than half of those under 55 report a great concern with being financially independent, while half of them admit concern with their ability to keep up with bills and weekly expenses.

The area of health/well-being appears to be a major preoccupation in the lives of older Americans. Specifically, more than half are very concerned with maintaining their independence physically in older age, compared with 39 percent of younger adults. Surprisingly, ability to contact someone in case of emergency is much more important among younger than older adults, with about 42 percent and 28 percent, respectively, reporting such a concern. Social and family-related issues are also of greater importance to younger adults. Older adults are not as preoccupied with taking care of their aging parents (since fewer are likely to have living parents), with only about 12 percent of them reporting such a concern, in comparison with 22 percent for younger adults. Nor do older people seem to be concerned a great deal with how close others feel toward them. Generally, social concerns are not a major issue in the lives of older Americans.

Two home-related topics examined are of equal significance. A large percentage (about 41 percent) of both groups appears to be concerned with home safety and security. The ability to find someone to do home or appliance repairs is not a major concern in general, but older people are more likely than their younger counterparts to report difficulty in locating a suitable person or company.

The need for information is relatively high among older adults. A large percentage of them express a great concern with getting useful information in general; of equal magnitude is the need for good financial, tax, or legal advice. Yet, these concerns do not appear to be confined to older Americans. Rather, younger people find this type of information of greater significance. Half of younger adults express concern with obtaining useful information on a variety of topics, while 45 percent of them show concern with getting good financial, tax, or legal advice.

The importance of leisure tends to receive low ratings among older adults. Barely one in five expresses a serious concern with finding means of enjoyment, while only one in ten expresses concern with an ability to attend special events and activities. Again, younger adults show a stronger orientation toward such leisure-related activities, with 31 percent and 17 percent of them expressing concern for the two leisure-related items, respectively, outscoring older adults.

Responses to items concerning daily activities are of equal magnitude among younger and older adults. A little over one-fourth of people in both groups express concern with shopping and running errands, and about one in five feels the same about fixing meals.

Problems

Needs can also be assessed by looking at problems experienced by older adults. To the extent that the aged person identifies a problem area, it is suggested that there is a need for solving that problem or a need for alternative ways of interaction with one's environment. Problems also tend to be unique to individuals in a given situation or social structure and vary in specificity.

One way of looking at general and specific problem areas is to identify older adults' activities of daily living that are key to maintaining their independence (e.g., walking, shopping, meal preparation). To the extent that older people experience difficulties carrying out these activities, specific problem areas can be identified.

In a survey of noninstitutionalized people age 55 or older conducted by the Gallup Organization, most respondents identified the following as problems (American Society on Aging 1987):

- opening medical packages
- reading product labels
- reaching high things
- fastening buttons, snaps, and zippers
- vacuuming and dusting
- going up and down stairs
- cleaning bathtubs and sinks
- washing and waxing floors
- putting clothes over one's head
- putting on shoes, socks, or stockings
- carrying purchases home
- using tools
- if something happened at home, no one would know
- using the shower or bathtub
- tying shoelaces, bows, and neckties
- moving around the house without slipping and falling

A rather similar approach to identifying problem areas is to identify situations that either limit or inhibit the individual's day-to-day functioning. For example, a recent study identified constraints across the life span serving as limiters and inhibitors (Nasar and Farokhpay 1985). Health reasons were identified by more than half (57.9%) of those over 75 years of age, compared with 23.9 percent of those between ages 61 and 75, and 8.9 percent among the 51 to 60 age group. Interestingly, lack of social contacts was perceived to be a limiting factor of equal magnitude among the 61 to 75 age group as well as among those 18 to 28 years of age, while the other age groups expressed a much lower concern. Similarly, health was the major inhibitor for the vast majority of those over 75 (80.0%) in comparison with the 61 to 75 age group (69.3%) and those in the 51 to 60 age category (48.5%). Surprisingly, safety problems, lack of money, and transportation did not surface either as limiters or as inhibitors.

Problems experienced by older adults may not be experienced by their younger counterparts, and the intensity of the same problem is likely to differ by other factors such as geographic location. E. Sherman and M. Brittain (1973) showed findings that point to the difficulties of elderly in urban areas in regard to mobility and transportation. These difficulties present problems in attempting to secure one basic necessity—food. D. Bauer and B. Warner (1978) stated that lack of transportation is a major problem for the rural elderly seeking employment.

On the other hand, other investigators report few differences in problems facing older people living in different locations. For example, Andrew Sofranko, Frederick C. Fliegel, and Nina Glasgow (1982–1983) found that problems experienced by both the urban and rural elderly are similar in type. In order of importance they are buying consumer goods, getting good medical care, making new friends, and joining clubs and organizations. Similarly, Richard C. Maurer, James A. Christenson, and Paul D. Warner (1980) examined perceived problems among elderly in rural and urban areas and concluded that few differences in perceived community services exist between (1) urban and rural elderly, with those in rural areas perceiving problems as more serious, and (2) the elderly's views and those of the rest of the population. Similar problems are also faced by people in different parts of the world when it comes to asking them about their perceptions of the marketplace (French et al. 1983).

Identification of specific problems in specific areas among older adults has also been the focus of several investigations. For example, one study of forty-six women age 65 and over in Stark County, Ohio, focused on their clothing needs. The study revealed that older women have difficulty purchasing clothing that fits properly, is comfortable and attractive, and is easy to put on. Recommendations were made based on the results of this investigation, such as clothing should be styled with front openings, gored or A-line skirts, larger armholes, lower necklines, and larger waistlines to accommodate body changes brought about by age (Pieper 1968).

Howard G. Schutz, Pamela C. Baird, and Glenn R. Hawkes (1979) identified specific problems among 309 older adults (age 45+) in several areas including finances, transportation, health care, food, and housing. Unfortunately, information on how these responses differ from those of younger age groups is not available in this study. As a result, one cannot be quite sure whether there are more or less important problems in relation to the rest of the population.

Fears

Needs are often expressed as fears. Deteriorating health is a primary, if not *the* primary, fear. A Yankelovich study (Markle Foundation 1988) identified loss of good health and mental acuity as major fears of age. A *USA Today* study also identified deteriorating health as a big fear (O'Driscoll 1987). When asked what they would do if they could no longer care for themselves, 22 percent of the 799 adults polled said "die." This fear was second only to "move into a nursing home" (32%). Although responses were not broken down by age, it is apparent that health is a big concern among older adults.

Particular fears of older Americans striving to be self-reliant and independent are the threat of medical emergency—that is, what to do in case of emergency and how to get help (Markle Foundation 1988)—and financial failure. Apparently, fear of physical, mental, and financial failure may render them "dependent," and institutionalization serves as official confirmation of their inadequacies.

Fear of crime is often thought to be a major preoccupation among the elderly population. However, statistics show that older adults are less likely to be victimized than younger people. Compared with people 65 years and older, people under 25 are robbed four times as often and assaulted seventeen times more often; people 25 to 49 are robbed twice as often and assaulted eight times more (Meddis and DeQuine 1987). The reason given for the perception that the elderly are victimized more often might be due to higher publicity on the part of the media. Reasons given for the lower victimization rate is that older people may have a higher level of fear and stay home more or do not expose themselves to conditions likely to favor victimization. Crime statistics do not take into account fraud against older adults.

Fear of crime can be reduced and security consciousness can be raised to make older people feel more at ease. Social integration has been found to have an adverse effect on the level of fear, and so does communication with the police (Lee 1983). Crime education could increase security-conscious behavior, but it might also increase the level of fear among the elderly (Norton and Courlander 1982). Fear may be higher in select segments of the population like those elderly living in urban areas and of certain ethnic backgrounds (Kahana and Felton 1977).

Expressed Interests

Needs can also be identified by examining areas of interest or attention of the aged person. For example, one survey found that the major interests of the retired are companionship, social activities, and a monitor system checking regularly on the retiree's health, safety, and security (Fishbein 1975). According to another study, approximately 15 percent of the elderly express an interest in learning new skills (Bauer and Warner 1978).

One problem in using expressed interest to identify the needs of older adults is that these people often dismiss their real needs or do not want to admit to others, even to themselves, that they have a particular need. For example, there is some indication that the oldest population makes a deliberate effort to dismiss health problems (Markle Foundation 1988).

Many of the interests expressed by older adults are not unique to them as a group. Quite often we see studies where both older and younger adults report similar levels of interests and activities (e.g., Yankelovich 1987). However, it is not clear whether the similarity in interest levels is due to lack of biophysical and psychosocial changes or to conscious efforts of older people to continue behaving like their younger counterparts. Lack of differences might also be due to cohort or socialization factors, making younger adults aware of activities (e.g., preventive health care, financial planning) that increase their independence and well-being throughout life, not just during the later years. For example, many younger Americans are caregivers to their aged relatives, and caregiving may increase their level of awareness of problems they may encounter in late life.

In evaluating differences in several dozen behaviors and activities between younger and older people, Daniel Yankelovich (1987) found that people 50 years of age and older, in comparison to those in the 39 to 49 age bracket, are more likely to:

- give high priority to gardening/landscaping, automobiles, and clothes
- give priority to entertaining relatives and friends at home
- express commitment to making more charitable contributions
- walk for fitness

Surprisingly, many of the comparisons between the two age groups did not show significant differences. This may be because the older group included respondents who feel and act as if they were in their 40s. Thus, the age groups chosen to be compared might affect the results; the more extreme the age groups, the greater the expected differences.

To summarize, although older adults' needs are likely to change in late life, specifying the nature of such needs and understanding reasons for changes are not easy tasks. Decision makers must be aware of the difficulties in identifying and working with needs, rather than try to ignore them.

SUMMARY OF PRESENT KNOWLEDGE AND PRACTICE

The discussion of various types of needs and methods for need assessment suggests several key points for consideration by those working in this area. First, with respect to their nature, the term *need* is a rather ambiguous concept, lacking clear definition and understanding. Needs are neither clearly defined nor delineated. Higher level and general types of needs may subsume lower level and more specific needs. Sets of needs can be identified in every area. General and specific needs can be observed in each specific field. Second, presence or absence of certain needs cannot be easily explained. Many needs are a direct outgrowth of biophysical and psychosocial changes associated with advancing age and can be understood in that context; others are based on structural factors and availability or awareness factors. Third, many needs of older adults are not fulfilled either because of the presence of factors that hinder their expression or due to the absence of factors that facilitate their manifestation into action.

Several methods are available for assessing needs of older adults. Although no particular method claims to be better than others, one must be aware of the differences in the results obtained depending upon the specific method used. When using self-reported procedures to identify needs, one must keep in mind that (1) older people may not accurately express their needs and (2) the reported needs are likely to vary by several respondent characteristics. Needs can also be uncovered simply by examining specific behaviors. Although not all behaviors are easily interpretable in the context of needs, they tend to reflect upon latent need structures. Present methods available for assessing needs vary widely, and there is little evidence to suggest that need assessment methods are presently adequate. Popular approaches to need derivation are those that either directly assess levels of needs (i.e., self-reported, structured approaches) or those that indirectly assume their presence by the level of interest in non-obligatory activities and in the older person's ability to perform obligatory activities independently.

Despite difficulties in working with needs, the area appears to be crucial to decisions concerning the development and marketing of products and services to the aging population. The following section gives examples of how needs can be used to design and market products and services, drawing from the author's consulting experiences and other successful cases.

DEVELOPING PRODUCTS AND SERVICES TO SATISFY NEEDS

Needs of older consumers can be used as bases for designing products and services, as well as communicating and distributing such offerings to the intended market. A useful way of using needs to develop various strategies is to analyze the needs of older consumers in the context of activities driven by such needs, or needs driven by activities (McMillan and Moschis 1985). To illustrate the former case, new services may be suggested as alternative solutions to activities driven by needs, which in turn are created by events. For example, a fall (event) can create a need (emergency—i.e., ability to reach help) that leads to activities (e.g., alert family, notify authorities), which can suggest alternative solutions (emergency-response systems). In this example, needs exist at all times and drive the activity that is stimulated by an event. Needs can also be stimulated by activities and can be driven by those activities. If a certain activity is not performed, the need does not exist. For instance, traveling to attend a conference or group meeting (activity) can be expensive and time consuming; it creates the need for less expensive and less time consuming ways to accomplish this purpose, and suggests alternative ways such as teleconferencing and video-conferencing.

Because aging during later stages in the life cycle is associated with biopsychosocial changes (events) as well as changes in lifestyles (activities), it appears useful to approach product-concept identification by assessing events and activities that are likely to develop or drive needs. While the distinction between events and activities may be difficult at times, one can think of events as being outside the person's immediate control while activities can be thought of as something a person has control over. Given this workable distinction, one can identify events associated with aging. Perhaps the most important types of events are those related to physiological changes in older people.

Research has delineated categories that relate to physiological limitations imposed by the normal aging process and the more common health problems that occur with age. Although such a classification may be somewhat arbitrary, it provides bases for addressing specific needs and activities that suggest products and services (existing or new) capable of satisfying them. For example, personal-hygiene-related needs suggest medical services, home maintenance services, and so on. There are other factors related to a person's stage in life—psychological and social factors as well as factors related to the physical environment in which the person lives—all likely to affect the older person's needs. For example, for those rural residents unable to operate personal vehicles, relative isolation makes certain needs significant (e.g., entertainment, shopping, health care, and emergency services). Using this approach, a major telecommunications company was able to develop and market a long list of products and services to satisfy various needs of older adults (McMillan and Moschis 1985). For example, the need to find a reliable repairman is most likely to be present among widows who had relied on their spouse to take care of home repairs. This group of older adults was particularly receptive to the idea of having the telephone company recommend and dispatch a certified repairman to take care of emergency repairs.

A final approach to gaining insights into the needs of mature adults uses problem identification to suggest required products or services as solutions. For example, one study (Fox 1980) identified the following major problems of the elderly:

1. Medicare abuse—less service provided than is reported.
2. Shortage of medical care in rural areas.
3. High insurance costs.
4. Home repair abuses—elderly must depend upon good faith of service people.
5. Utility costs.
6. Lack of awareness of consumer rights—perpetration of fraud on elderly is often not prosecuted.

Given these problems, a number of solutions can then be suggested. For example, home health care can be suggested instead of hospital care to reduce costs of care. The Department of Health and Human Services indicates that the average home care visit costs about $50 compared to the average daily cost of a hospital stay of $300 (McMillan and Moschis 1985). Another example of this approach is found in the area of telecommunications. After a study found "crank and obscene calls" were among the list of common problems consumers experience, this problem was solved by developing call-tracing services (McMillan and Moschis 1985).

PRODUCT DEVELOPMENT BASED ON NEEDS: AN ILLUSTRATION

New product development is a process that takes into account consumer needs and wants, company resources, and environmental factors such as legal and competitive forces. This section discusses an approach to new product development for older consumers. The process is illustrated with actual data used in developing and testing new products and services. The step-by-step process begins with research and ends with a suggested list of products and services for older consumers.

The suggested research plan employs two types of research designs: exploratory research and a large-scale survey.

Exploratory Research

Exploratory research consists of activities conducted over a period of time in four stages:

1. Identification of mature consumer needs in the marketplace.
2. Generation of concepts to satisfy the identified needs.
3. Screening of concepts and combining the ideas for concept testing/development.
4. Testing or developing/modifying concepts.

Need Identification

This stage involves analyzing published and proprietary sources of information and developing a list of needs associated with biophysical and psychological changes in later stages of life. Based on information presented, the identified needs are summarized as follows:

1. *Physiological needs*, due to a decrease in the ability to:
   a. hear (higher frequency sounds);
   b. see (decreased focusing speed, sensitivity to light, distortion of colors, visual deficiency, and reduction of total field of vision);
   c. taste and distinguish among substances;
   d. grip and hold;
   e. smell;
   f. touch, feel pain; and
   g. remember (short-term memory loss)
   and due to:
   h. chronic conditions: heart, disease, high blood pressure, arthritis, severe physical impairment/handicap/institutionalization.
2. *Companionship/interpersonal needs*, as a result of social isolation and loss of face-to-face interaction.
3. *Information needs* regarding increasingly important issues (health, Social Security, housing, finances, local affairs, etc.), combined with growing loss of social interaction.
4. *Entertainment needs*, due to increasing leisure time, retirement in rural areas, and immobility.
5. *Domestic assistance needs*, due to physical impairment, isolation, and need for convenience. Specific needs related to:
   a. shopping;
   b. cooking;
   c. bill paying;
   d. mailing/picking up of packages;
   e. self-diagnosis;
   f. legal and financial;
   g. home management; and
   h. home repair.
6. *Need to stay active* by:
   a. helping others through volunteerism;
   b. continued learning (formal and informal); and
   c. postponing retirement or reentering the labor market.
7. *Survival and safety/protection needs*:
   a. home security;

  b. health/personal; and
  c. financial security (due to fixed income and inflation).

Concept Generation

Concept generation is based on the premise that various types of needs developing in the aging individual can be satisfied with products/services developed specifically for older consumers as well as with specific methods of promotion and product or service delivery—that is, marketing approaches. The development of new (or modified) product concepts in our research, which is used to illustrate this process, was guided by two methodologies: brainwriting and synectics using a large number of experts from various industries.

Brainwriting is a silent written generation of ideas by a group of selected individuals (Van Gundy 1983). The key informant approach was used to select "experts" with different skills in various fields. These individuals were presented with the entire list of needs identified and were asked to suggest products or ideas that would satisfy each particular need (see Appendix A).

Synectics is a creativity technique for idea generation (Osborn 1963). Based on the results from brainwriting, the participants of these sessions suggested and explored additional ideas. The participants were identified using the key informant or sociometric method as "creative" and "knowledgeable" individuals regarding the consumption needs of older adults. Approximately 200 new concepts or ideas for product and service offerings capable of satisfying specific needs were suggested by participants of brainwriting and synectics sessions. Many of these ideas were based on new or emerging technologies.

The development of new concepts for better marketing of products/services to older consumers was guided by previous research and brainstorming sessions with approximately 40 graduate students taking classes on Buyer Behavior at Georgia State University. Over 100 different hypotheses (marketing tactics and specific implications) were identified based on the list of needs and previous research (see Appendix B).

Screening and Combining Concepts

This stage involves the consolidation of the various concepts generated based on criteria such as concept similarity, viability, cost versus potential market size, and available technology. The main objective at this stage is to identify those concepts that can be realistically implemented given the available or emerging technologies, expected potential market, cost, consumer ability to buy, and legal/political constraints. The assistance of experts from different backgrounds is solicited in order to perform this task.

By screening and combining the concepts in our example, the original list was reduced to approximately 100 new product/service ideas and nearly 50 hypotheses regarding business tactics aimed at marketing products and services, in line with theory and research on older consumers.

Concept Modification/Development

Most of the "new" product concepts required no further refinement or definition, since it was a question of (1) execution and (2) customer reaction/acceptance (test marketing). However, for some ideas about new (emerging) products and services, it was necessary to undertake a pretesting for better formulation or modification of the concepts to make them more suitable to older customer needs. To accomplish this objective, the most promising of the 100 new product/service ideas, particularly those based on new or emerging technologies, were presented to participants of several focus groups. The results of these sessions suggested not only ways of modifying and improving the proposed concepts, but also the development of additional product and service ideas and the elimination of others. The final list of viable new product and service ideas included a wide variety of products and services ranging from home-diagnostic services (e.g., health, general maintenance problems) to various forms of security and alarm systems; from telecommunication equipment and services to financial and billing services; from information, entertainment, and educational services to appliances for the physically impaired; and to various learning clubs and centers for older adults.

Survey

The second phase of the suggested plan for new product development and marketing involves a survey. To accomplish this objective in our case study, a nationwide mail survey was conducted. From the large number of concepts generated and retained, the survey could obtain the older person's reaction to only a manageable number of such concepts that appeared to lend themselves to brief and accurate descriptions in a mail questionnaire.

A sample of 6,000 individuals age 55 and over was randomly drawn from the 50 states, in proportion to the population and age-group distribution of each state. Thus, if a state had 1 percent of the total U.S. population, the number of subjects from that state was 60 (1% of 6,000). The distribution of age subsamples within each state also represented the age composition of the population in that state. For example, if 60 names were to be drawn from the 55-and-over age group of a given state and 50 percent of the state's older (55+) population was between the ages of 55 and 64, the subsample of individuals age 55 to 64 drawn from that state was 30. Another sample of 2,000 individuals age 25 to 54 was drawn using the same approach. These individuals were surveyed for comparison ("control") purposes.

The names and addresses of 8,000 individuals were obtained from R. L. Polk & Co., a nationally known mailing list supplier that specializes in compilation of names by age group. The procedure involved (1) specification of subsample parameters (in our case, size of sample by state and age group based on census data) and (2) selection of subjects using random sampling procedures.

The questionnaire consisted of two major parts. The first included questions designed to obtain information on dependent variables—that is, respondents' perceptions of, and attitudes toward, various types of new and emerging product/service concepts, as well as orientations toward marketing practices in the areas of promotion, product development, pricing and distribution (see Appendix C). The second part of the instrument was used to obtain sociodemographic information, measures of needs and lifestyles, and use of sources of information.

Many of the measures that were included in the questionnaire had been developed and used in previous studies, especially measures related to marketing practices (most of the demographic variables, and attitudes toward high-tech products, brands, stores, and prices). The length of the questionnaire was six pages. This length allowed the use of a relatively large type size (eleven point) to assist the older adults in the sample who might have had vision problems.

Of the approximately fifty new product or service ideas identified and screened via exploratory research (described earlier), approximately half offered adequate representation (several product/service ideas were closely related). These product/service concepts had been derived from a wide variety of identified need categories; they were pretested and screened. The final list of approximately twenty products were pretested, and thirteen of those that were the easiest to describe in writing were included in the questionnaire. About half of these products and services were simple, and half were complex, with the latter type involving multilevel abstract relationships (see Appendix D).

In addition to measuring the respondents' perceived desirability of the new products and services, the questionnaire also asked respondents to indicate whether they were aware of, perceived interest in, or presently used a number of relatively new products/services on the market. This list included five products and services related to major types of needs (discussed earlier): cable television (entertainment and information), electronic funds transfer (EFT, security/protection), automatic teller machines (ATMs, domestic assistance), Custom Calling Telephone Services (CCTS—e.g., "call waiting") (companionship/interpersonal), and cordless phone (physiological). The products on this list were used to (1) validate responses obtained on the longer product/service list (intentions to use/buy), (2) compare the results of those of previous studies (e.g., Gilly and Ziethaml 1985; Prisuta and Kriner 1985), and (3) compare usage of recent innovations with interest in proposed product/service concepts to determine demand likelihood for each specific product or service concept.

The characteristics of the nearly 1,000 older respondents age 55 and over who responded are shown in Appendix E. The results of the survey are reported in Chapter 5 (market segments), Chapter 6 (information sources), Chapter 7 (orientations toward products), Chapter 8 (adoption of new products and services), Chapter 9 (orientations toward retail outlets), Chapter 10 (responses to promotional practices), and Chapter 11 (responses to age-targeted marketing strategies).

4

Segmenting and Targeting the Mature Market

The mature market presents challenges to marketers because much of the information about the marketplace is based on younger consumers, who tend to differ from older consumers in many important ways. For example, U.S. Department of Labor surveys show a great variation in spending on various types of products and services by age of householders (U.S. Bureau of Labor Statistics 1989). Of greater significance to marketers, however, is the heterogeneity of the mature market. Research shows that the older a person gets, the more he or she differs from others. This finding poses a problem to marketers who are developing strategies for mass markets, and also offers an opportunity for those appealing to groups of older consumers sharing similar characteristics.

Because of differences in attitudes, values, and behaviors among older consumers, a "shotgun" approach to marketing does not appear to be an effective strategy. A given marketing strategy may be effective with one category of older adults, while other groups of the mature market will find the same offerings less attractive. A more effective strategy to reach a heterogeneous market is to match company offerings with the needs of subgroups. Doing this calls for market segmentation and target marketing. Market segmentation refers to subdividing the market into several groupings, with each group being recognized for its preferences regarding products/services and methods of delivery. Target marketing refers to the development of a different viable marketing mix for each of the segments.

This chapter first discusses issues of market segmentation, as well as alternative segmentation models. Next, it evaluates the efficacy of existing

This chapter is adapted from Moschis (1992b).

models in designing effective strategy; it presents a new way of segmenting the mature consumer market and validates the model using data from our national study. Finally, implications of the segmentation model for marketers are discussed.

MARKET SEGMENTATION

Rationale for Segmentation

Segmentation analysis is based on the assumption that individuals differ in perceptions, attitudes, and consumption behavior, but these differences are not entirely idiosyncratic. That is, there should be subgroupings of the older population whose members share similarities but differ markedly from members of other subgroupings.

Market segmentation appears to be an effective strategic tool for addressing the mature market, not only because this market is highly diversified but also because of its size. The U.S. Bureau of the Census estimates that there are approximately 53 million people age 55 and older and 31 million age 65 and older. Subsegments of these groups are likely to be sizeable as well, justifying the development of different strategies to reach them. Finally, segmentation provides opportunities for efficiency and specialization. Simply, a company can achieve better results by designing marketing programs that match the needs of specific subsegments and by developing a market niche than by attempting to reach all consumers with the same marketing program.

Bases for Segmentation

While segmentation analysis appears to be an easy concept to implement, it is surrounded by problems and controversies. There are presently numerous ways of subdividing the market, and no two ways are likely to produce similar results. For example, the mature market has been segmented into age groupings such as 55 to 64, 65 to 74, and 75 or older (Lazer 1986). It has also been segmented according to lifestyles using VALS (Values and Life Styles) (Gollub and Javitz 1989). Because segmentation is based on the premise that subgroupings differ, any factor that shows variability in behavior in the marketplace can conceivably be used as a basis for developing subgroups. This wide choice poses a problem in terms of what the best criteria are and how many criteria should be used. For example, is just one criterion such as age or lifestyle sufficient, or could better results be obtained by considering another criterion or several factors simultaneously?

While segmentation analysis of the mature market is usually based on a single factor such as age, the use of multiple factors appears to be a more viable approach for a number of reasons. First, differences in consumer responses among older people are not likely to be the result of any specific factor. Changes or differences in behavior in late life are usually the manifestation of different types of aging processes. Because people age differently, and aging is inherently multidimensional, a wide variability in attitudes, behaviors, and abilities exists. People age biologically, psychologically, socially, and even spiritually, and these aging processes are manifested in differences in attitudes and behavior even among people of the same age.

Second, the use of any single criterion for segmentation not only is unlikely to capture the wide variability in such processes but also may not be appropriate or the most viable criterion. For example, consider personality traits used by many psychographic or lifestyle segmentation models. Several decades of research by Bernice Neugarten, a noted gerontologist, produced findings suggesting that personality changes little after age 30 (Barrow and Smith 1983). This finding is also confirmed by a Daniel Yankelovich (1987) study for *Modern Maturity* magazine, which shows few differences in lifestyles between younger and older adults. Thus, one does not expect to find variability in personality in late life, and therefore personality and lifestyles may not be sound bases for segmenting the mature market since they have been weak predictors of consumer behavior in general (Novak and MacEvoy 1990). Such factors do not adequately capture psychological aging of the individual, and so other psychological factors such as cognitive ability and subjective age (how old a person feels/thinks he or she is) might prove more effective.

Finally, we must use knowledge accumulated over several decades in the consumer field. This type of information suggests that consumer responses cannot be attributed simply to one factor based on one set of assumptions. Rather, practitioners must base their decisions on information from several disciplines. For nearly half a century gerontologists and consumer researchers have accumulated data that show that demographic characteristics such as age are not good predictors of human behavior in general and consumer behavior in particular (Moschis 1990). While gerontologists have dismissed age as a useful factor in explaining behavior in late life, consumer behavior researchers often cannot explain age differences in consumer responses. For example, they cannot say with certainty whether such differences are due to age per se or due to factors associated with age such as lifestyles, education, or social and environmental (cohort) effects. This prompted marketers to go beyond demographics and seek explanations in the person's "psychographics," an approach developed in the late 1960s that has recently waned in popularity as marketers and researchers have increasingly realized its unscientific bases and inability to explain consumer behavior (Bernstein 1978).

In sum, understanding consumer behavior in late life appears to be essential not only for segmenting the mature market but also in deciding how to better target it. Present segmentation models can segment the older consumer market, but they provide little or no information on how to effectively reach the desired subsegments. This is because our ability to predict market response depends on how well we can explain market behavior (a principle of science).

GERONTOGRAPHICS

Gerontographics (author's term) is an approach that acknowledges individual differences in aging processes as well as differences in type of aging dimensions that occur in late life. It attempts to gain insight into human behavior in late life by recognizing the multifaceted aspects of the aging process, and it considers consumer behavior to be a manifestation of these multidimensional processes and circumstances that people experience in late life.

Gerontographics is an approach similar to that of psychographics or lifestyles, but it focuses exclusively, and in much greater detail, on older adults' needs, attitudes, lifestyles, and behaviors. It differs from psychographics in a number of ways. First, gerontographics is a more comprehensive approach in that it considers the multiplicity of dimensions relevant to aging in late life. Besides psychological factors, which are the core bases in lifestyle models (e.g., VALS 2, List of Values [LOV]), gerontographics also considers factors associated with biological aging as well as social and experiential aging. Second, the approach takes into consideration various external circumstances or events in late life that can produce variability in older adults' behavior. Third, the number of subgroupings (segments) and their corresponding names are derived or specified on an *a priori* basis, based on our knowledge about human behavior in late life. By contrast, the psychographics and lifestyles approaches normally derive segments after the data have been gathered, and the number and names of subgroupings are likely to differ across researchers or studies. For example, studies using psychographics and personality have yielded different conclusions about the numbers and names of subgroupings of the aged market, although they have used similar methods (e.g., Gollub and Javitz 1989; Goldring & Company 1987). The marketer still must decide whether psychographics is a viable approach, which psychographics or lifestyles model is best, and why.

Gerontographics as an approach to market segmentation seeks improvement over other approaches in three ways: (1) by acknowledging the scientifically based claim in a large number of disciplines (e.g., social gerontology) that no single theory or type of variable can adequately explain behavior in late life—that is, similarities and differences of the mature market; (2) by offering explanation on why there should be a specific number of subsegments, as well as why older individuals in these groupings behave differently; and (3) by demonstrating that the derived segmentation model is more useful to marketers than are models based on limited types of variables.

In summary, gerontographics is based on the premise that the observed similarities and differences in the consumer behavior of older adults are the outcome of several social, psychological, biophysical lifetime events and other environmental factors, all affecting the aged person differently. The derivation of mature market subsegments is based on the premise that those older people who experience similar circumstances in late life (defined by the person's gerontographic characteristics) are likely to exhibit similar patterns of consumer behavior, patterns that differ from those of other older adults experiencing different sets of circumstances, that is, having different gerontographic characteristics.

Gerontographic Segments

The 53 million adults age 55 and over can be grouped into four gerontographic segments: healthy hermits (20 million), ailing outgoers (18 million), frail recluses (8 million), and healthy indulgers (7 million). (They can also be grouped into four need-based segments, as described in Appendix F.) Individuals in each segment can be described on the basis of several characteristics, including demographics, consumption-related needs, and how they respond to companies' marketing efforts. These characteristics were not used to form the four segments but are useful in describing the segments and their consumer behavior. We will only use a small number of such characteristics to illustrate the heterogeneity of the derived segments. Table 4.1 shows needs and concerns of older Americans classified into four gerontographic groups, while Table 4.2 provides information about their behavior in the marketplace based on responses given to questions in our national survey. Percentage differences of approximately ±7 percent between two segments indicate a significant difference ($p < .05$ level). A table is provided in Appendix G to help the reader determine the stability and significance of percentages reported.

Healthy Hermits

Individuals in this segment tend to have the following characteristics: they are in good health, psychologically withdrawn from society, concerned with day-to-day tasks, and tend to be employed. They have few social contacts and little interest in staying active.

This group has relatively few consumption-related needs and expresses the fewest concerns. Older consumers in this group tend to have a negative attitude toward technological innovations. Healthy hermits are relatively more likely to pay off the entire balance on their charge accounts and to

Table 4.1
Consumption-Related Needs by Gerontographic Clusters (percentage "concerned a lot")

	Healthy Hermits	Ailing Outgoers	Frail Recluses	Healthy Indulgers
Money				
Being able to keep up with bills and weekly expenses	7.34	55.56	31.45	32.18
Being financially Independent	17.78	73.51	43.41	64.55
Health/Well-Being				
Being able to contact someone in case of emergency	4.72	52.81	29.07	33.50
Social/Family				
Having to take care of your aging parents	4.97	21.73	8.58	13.91
Feeling that no one cares for you	14.35	33.93	24.40	18.79
Home				
Having your home/apartment burned or burglarized	24.65	61.27	48.65	30.45
Finding someone to do home or appliance repairs	15.13	32.04	24.74	17.95
Information				
Getting useful information on things that affect you	16.72	54.52	37.43	60.23
Getting good financial, tax, or legal advice	20.31	48.46	35.46	46.25
Leisure				
Finding ways to enjoy yourself (like travel and entertainment)	3.53	38.62	3.49	43.01
Being able to attend special events or activities	2.58	22.83	4.02	14.42
Daily Activities				
Being able to do your shopping and run errands	7.11	51.62	25.06	33.31
Being able to fix your meals	1.70	41.48	18.35	25.76

have difficulty sticking to a savings plan. This group tends to be the least responsive to marketing strategies based on age.

Ailing Outgoers

Individuals in this group tend to be health conscious and in relatively poor physical condition. However, they are socially active, unlikely to

Table 4.2
Consumer Behavior of Older Americans by Gerontographic Clusters
(percentage "strongly/somewhat agree")

	Healthy Hermits	Ailing Outgoers	Frail Recluses	Healthy Indulgers
Responses to Age-Based Strategies				
Companies should offer more discounts to older than to younger adults	40.3	65.9	61.5	50.4
I like advertisements that show products especially for older people	17.8	36.7	25.7	26.8
Responses to Promotional Strategies				
I am attracted to special displays in a store	29.3	38.9	32.4	42.5
I usually watch the advertisements for announcement of sales	72.9	79.7	69.6	70.1
New Products				
I like to try something new every time I am in the store	11.8	16.4	8.8	15.0
I try to learn as much as I can about a new product/service before buying or using it	76.2	81.0	68.9	77.2
Dis/satisfaction with Products/Services				
I sometimes wish I could get my money back for some things I bought	66.0	82.6	77.7	83.5
I often find packages and containers difficult to open	60.5	67.2	73.0	63.0
High Tech Products				
Using calculators, computers, and other electronic gadgets is usually too confusing to bother with	21.1	31.5	36.5	36.2
Older people should learn to use electronic gadgets and services that can make their life easier	66.7	76.8	65.5	77.9
Payments Systems				
I like to pay cash for most things I buy	74.2	85.8	78.4	69.3
I seldom pay off the entire balance on my monthly statements of my charge accounts	9.0	21.2	14.9	18.1

change their lifestyle because of their age, interested in learning and doing new things, and retired. Ailing outgoers are a prime market for consumer products and services. They have strong needs for information and domestic-assistance products and services. They are very concerned with financial matters and desire to be financially independent. A major psychological characteristic of this group is concern with security of health, home, and assets.

Ailing outgoers' consumer behavior patterns differ from those of other subsegments. They tend to pay cash for products and services, and they are less likely to pay off their monthly charge account balance than individuals in all other segments combined. Individuals in this group tend to report favorable attitudes toward age-based marketing strategies, such as products and promotional strategies for "older people."

Frail Recluses

Mature adults falling into this category tend to be in poor health, inactive, socially isolated, and psychologically withdrawn from society. They are more likely to be retired than employed, and they are more security conscious than those in the other three groups. Although concerns with security are confined to physical and home safety, as opposed to, for example, financial security (a main concern of ailing outgoers), they desire mainly physical protection.

Frail recluses are more likely to report difficulty opening packages and containers than are the other groups, but they are less likely to seek product information prior to a purchase. However, they are not likely to admit that they cannot use product information.

Healthy Indulgers

These mature adults are in rather good health and are independent, active, and relatively wealthy. They are socially "engaged," want the most out of life, and are not hesitant to indulge themselves. Healthy indulgers have a strong need for selective information; they are likely to pursue leisure activities and to be involved in volunteerism and other community activities.

Healthy indulgers are attracted to in-store displays more than any other group. They are also likely to report favorable attitudes toward technology. Finally, healthy indulgers tend to be the group least likely to pay cash for products and services, and, therefore, they are relatively high users of credit.

The four groups of older adults are at four different stages in late life (see Figure 4.1). The first stage includes healthy indulgers. Mature Americans who are at this stage are closest to the stage in which most baby boomers are found. The major difference between mature people who experience this stage and baby boomers is that the former group is better off financially and settled career-wise, with their main focus on enjoying life rather than trying to "make it in life." Opposite to this is the life stage occupied by frail recluses. At some earlier point in time they may have been healthy indulgers, although stages are age-irrelevant. Many frail recluses may have gone through the intermediate life stages experienced by healthy hermits and ailing outgoers. The former group is relatively more

Figure 4.1
Life Stages of the Mature Market

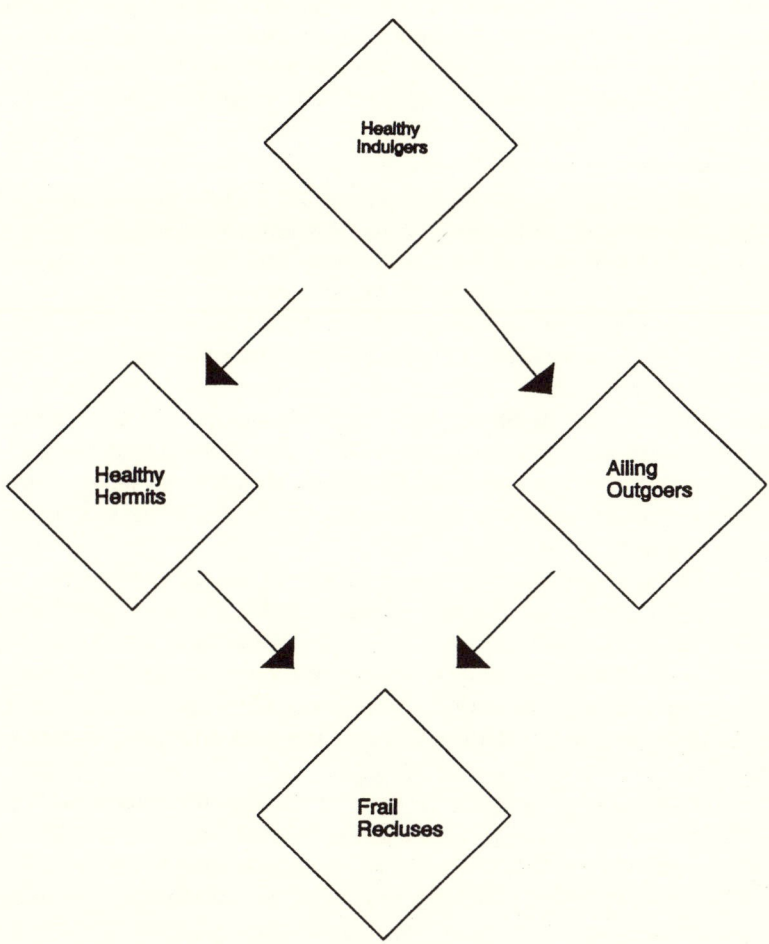

Note: Arrows indicate that people may move to the next stage in life due to physiological, psychological, and social aging.

socially withdrawn and healthy but secluded, while the latter is still active and likely to maintain high self-esteem despite health problems. Furthermore, healthy hermits are concerned with day-to-day tasks and likely to deny their "old age" status, while ailing outgoers have internalized many of their families, and, while they try to make the best out of life, they are preoccupied with their physical and financial independence and well-being. Thus, people in late life can move from one stage to another. Although such changes may occur over time or may be abrupt (e.g., retirement or stroke, respectively), the processes or "flows" are relatively age-irrelevant because they may begin at any age in life or may never be experienced.

While there are no age differences across the four segments, these groups differ across several domains that define life stages. Healthy indulgers have experienced the fewest life events (e.g., retirement, loss of spouse, chronic health conditions) that may contribute to the person's psychological and social aging. As a result, they are the group most likely to behave like younger consumers. Healthy hermits are likely to have experienced life events (e.g., death of spouse) that have affected their self-concept and self-worth and have forced them into psychological and social withdrawal. Many of them resent the fact that they have been forced into isolation and are expected to behave like old people. On the other hand, ailing outgoers are the group most likely to maintain positive self-esteem and self-concept, despite life events that demand changes in their lifestyles such as retirement, death of spouse, and health problems. Unlike healthy hermits, many ailing outgoers accept the "old age" status but refuse to change their lifestyles, acknowledging their limitations but still trying to get the most out of life. Finally, frail recluses are likely to have accepted their older age status and have adjusted their lifestyles to reflect biophysical declines and changes in social roles. In order to cope with these detrimental changes in late life they have become spiritually stronger.

While only few factors are used to describe the life-stage model, it is based on several dozen variables that have been found to affect behaviors and attitudes in late life. The model acknowledges individual differences in aging processes as well as differences in types of aging that occur in late life. It attempts to gain insight into human behavior in late life by recognizing the multifaceted aspects of the aging process, and considers consumer behavior to be a manifestation of these multidimensional processes and circumstances people experience in late life—that is, their gerontographic characteristics.

The four life stages are not only suggested by research in the field of aging and social sciences but are also confirmed as better predictors of marketplace behavior. When they are compared to segments based on age, cognitive age, and psychographics, all of which tend to capture single dimensions of aging, the four life stage segments give significantly different responses to a large number of marketing offerings and strategies. For example, a study conducted by the author for the American Association of Retired Persons (AARP) Andrus Foundation (reported in detail later in Chapter 8) found that nearly twice as many ailing outgoers as healthy hermits (61.4% versus 33.7%) would use a medical ID card that can be electronically read in case of emergency to provide medical staff useful health information. Healthy indulgers were found to be twice as likely as frail recluses (21.3% versus 11.5%) to prefer directories of phone numbers that can be dialed for prerecorded information on various topics. Preferences did not differ by age for the two products in the same study. Two-thirds of ailing outgoers said they would like to see companies offering more senior discounts, compared with just 40 percent of healthy hermits. Again, there were no age differences in responses to senior discounts.

In summary, the life-stage model is based on the assumption that the consumer behavior of older adults is the outcome of several biophysical, social, psychological, and lifetime events and other environmental factors, all of which affect the older person differently. The derivation of older consumer market subsegments is based on the premise that those older people who experience similar circumstances in late life are likely to show similar patterns of consumer behavior, patterns that differ from those of other older adults facing different sets of circumstances.

It should be emphasized that older consumers' responses to various marketing stimuli and strategies are likely to vary across products and services, reflecting the needs, attitudes, and lifestyle of each segment. For example, the groups that want to maintain their active lifestyles (healthy indulgers and ailing outgoers) are those in greater need of information on health-related issues, as shown in their propensity to read print media (newspaper and magazine ads, brochures/newsletters) that contain large amounts of updated information on health. On the other hand, the four groups do not differ much in their preferences for the same types of sources for food/beverage and fast-food products because such products in general are not as sensitive to aging processes in later life. However, when preferences for specific food products sensitive to some aging domains (e.g., health) are considered, the four groups are also likely to differ, with a higher percentage of ailing outgoers (47.8%) preferring dietary programs or dietary meals than frail recluses (32.8%) and healthy hermits (31.7%).

Similar observations can be made with respect to a number of other marketing factors, such as responses to ads of products targeted primarily at older people. For example, because older people are much heavier consumers of prescription drugs than younger adults, people in certain segments may be more or less sensitive to age stereotypes and the age of spokespersons in ads. Thus, older adults most likely to notice the age of the spokespersons in pharmacy store ads are those most likely to be the heaviest consumers of drugs (ailing outgoers and frail recluses). However, for products or services such as travel, the demand of which is fairly uniform across age groups, there are no significant group differences in perceptions of ads appealing to any specific age group. Therefore older and younger persons may be equally used as spokespersons.

Specific patronage motives differ not only across segments but also across types of products or services purchased, with such differences reflecting the aging dimensions describing each group. For example, the groups most likely to be socially and psychologically withdrawn (healthy hermits and frail recluses) are also likely to have fewer consumption needs, especially for discretionary consumption, than the more active groups. Thus, for a discretionary purchase, such as a travel package, patronage motives such as price, selection, advice of others, and past satisfaction with travel-package vendors differ across the four groups, with the most active group (healthy indulgers) considering these factors the most. However, for consumption of nondiscretionary (necessity) products, such as food items, patronage motives are not as sensitive to the underlying dimensions of the four life stages. Older people tend to patronize food stores as frequently as younger people and, therefore, are equally active in their shopping for such products.

To summarize, marketers of products and services should be aware that the life-stage model may fit some products better than others. Findings derived from analysis of consumer responses to marketing factors in one industry would not apply to other industries, suggesting the need for industry-specific gerontographic segmentation and marketing-response models for greater effectiveness.

IMPLICATIONS AND USEFULNESS

The gerontographics segmentation model was developed with two main objectives in mind: (1) to build a model that reflects current scientific knowledge in various disciplines about human behavior in late life, and (2) to offer marketers a scientifically based tool useful not only for making better predictions about the marketplace, but also for helping them understand why older adults behave in the ways they do. With such information, marketers should be in a better position to design effective strategies.

"One-type-variable" segmentation may be effective in some cases, as in the case of using health (presence of ailments) to segment the market for drugs, but it may not be applicable in many others. For example, the purchase of many products (e.g., retirement communities, household appliances) is likely to be the outcome of elaborate decision-making processes including the influence of household or family members. In such instances, psychological factors, which form the bases for other segmentation tools (e.g., VALS 2), may not be good predictors of the older person's behavior because they do not take into consideration the psychological profiles of other participants in the decision.

Gerontographics, on the other hand, is a holistic approach that takes into account the various structural circumstances that define the person's relationship with others in the social system. It is not limited to demographic or psychological factors but consists of an integrated system of variables that are used to represent the perplexity of forces that shape the older person's behavior in the marketplace.

Another benefit of this approach is that it helps market strategists go beyond the basic information provided by most segmentation models—that is, the mere description of the viable segments for a product or service. Once marketers identify prime prospects, they want to know how to target them and whether they should develop different strategies to reach different groups. They need to know not only the characteristics of those who are most likely to buy a product or service, but also how these consumers respond to various offerings of the firm. Present segmentation models are useful primarily in identifying older consumers who are likely to be good prospects for a given product, but they provide little or no information on the responses to marketing strategies and specific tactics. Besides identifying the characteristics of the potential customer, the model presented seeks to provide information crucial to market segmentation and targeting; it tells the decision maker how people in various segments respond to marketing strategies of the firm.

Gerontographics can offer information on response elasticities of the firm's marketing variables. (These elasticities can be examined by inspecting the coefficients of marketing variables in the discriminant model; see Appendix F.) This type of information could help marketers decide how to reach customers in each of the four segments with the most effective marketing mix—that is, how to allocate their marketing effort. For example, age-based marketing strategies would be most effective in reaching ailing outgoers but relatively less effective in appealing to healthy hermits.

Finally, the gerontographics database can be used in concert with other databases. Marketers looking for a particular gerontographic segment can use mass media, information on product usage, and zip code data unique to each segment to obtain more detailed information. Information on older Americans' media use habits, purchasing patterns, credit use, geographic location, and lifestyles is also available on other systems such as Mediamark Research, Inc. (MRI), PRIZM, SMRB, Arbitron, EQUIFAX, and VALS, which contain more specific information in several areas (e.g., radio listening, brand preferences). Furthermore, subscribers to these systems can identify the distribution of gerontographic types within clusters. A marketer who is targeting the "Money and Brains" cluster from Clarita's PRIZM, for example, can find out which gerontographic types dominate it: healthy hermits, ailing outgoers, frail recluses, or healthy indulgers. By adding this new dimension, marketers will be in a better position not only to identify viable segments, but also to determine the appropriate strategies in product development, advertising, pricing, sales promotion, and distribution. This new system of matching mature-consumer responses to marketing offerings can enhance the appeal of existing databases.

PART III

ANALYZING MARKET BEHAVIOR

5

Consumption and Financial Practices of Older Americans

Money management practices of older adults help us understand several aspects of their consumer behavior. Saving and spending patterns of older consumers tend to affect their expenditure patterns in specific consumption areas such as food, housing, and transportation. However, little is known about the factors that affect these behaviors and their motivations. Economic models do not explain consumer behavior very well. For example, according to the life cycle hypothesis, baby boomers are expected to save relatively more, and the elderly to draw down their assets. But analysis of census and survey data shows exactly the opposite (Gibler 1990; Reiner 1990).

The purpose of this chapter is to present data helpful in answering questions about general aspects of the older person's consumption and financial practices. For example, how do demographic factors affect the older person's consumer behavior with respect to spending and money-management practices? Can alternative explanations based on lifestyles and other factors related to the aging process provide answers to consumption and financial practices of older Americans? What methods of payment do older people prefer? Are older people possessing certain characteristics more likely to prefer certain methods? Previous research is first presented, followed by findings from our national study aimed at answering these questions. Finally, marketing implications of the research findings are discussed.

SAVING

Researchers at the University of Pennsylvania, after extensive analyses of the U.S. Bureau of Labor Statistics' *Consumer Expenditure Survey* data from 1960 to 1986, concluded that the elderly tend more to save than to spend (Moschis 1992a). Baby boomers, on the contrary, are on a consumption binge into middle age. The 1986 Survey of Consumer Finances by the Federal Reserve Board provides insights into the saving behavior of various age groups (U.S. Bureau of the Census 1990). The survey found that the average household savings in the United States over a three-year period (1983–1986) was $24,402. Households headed by people age 45 to 54 saved the most ($46,606), followed by those age 55 to 64 ($39,392) and 65 and over ($33,867). However, on a per capita basis the age-group ranking was the opposite ($16,071, $17,126, and $17,824, respectively). As a share of total household savings, 21.3 percent of the total amount was saved by those in the 65-and-over category, while those in the 55 to 64 bracket contributed 20.9 percent. Thus, those 55 and older accounted for approximately 42 percent of all savings realized during the three-year period. A *USA Today* (1985) survey found older Americans to have the most savings and investments (excluding real estate)—62 percent of the 65-and-over age group had $10,000 and more, compared with 53 percent of the 50 to 64 age group and 39 percent of the 35 to 49 age group indicating this amount of investment. In the same study, the percentage of the respondents in the three age groups who indicated saving/investing 10 percent or more of their income in the past twelve months were 24 percent, 30 percent, and 24 percent, respectively. Thus, even during late life a substantial number of older Americans save a large portion of their available income.

SPENDING

In 1989, households headed by individuals age 55 or older spent a total of $730 billion on goods and services, or 27 percent of expenditures of all U.S. households. Spending by older adults varies widely with age, depending upon whether one considers spending on a household or per capita basis. When one examines spending on a per household basis, the 55 to 64 age group is estimated to spend a little more (3 percent) than the national average, according to the 1989 *Consumer Expenditure Survey* by the U.S. Bureau of Labor Statistics. The spending figures for the 65 to 74 and 75-and-over groups are 24 percent and 43 percent *less* than the national average, respectively.

On the other hand, when spending is examined on a per capita basis, the mature person (55 and over) spends 10 percent more than the national average. With respect to per capita spending among different age groups, the 55 to 64 group spends 16 percent more than the average; the figures for the 65 to 74 and 75-and-over adults are 4 percent more and 7 percent less, respectively. Thus, the propensity to spend declines with age. Perhaps older adults do not have as many expenses as younger adults. Another explanation might be a learned inclination to hold on to their money because it makes them feel more secure. Older adults, especially those who were affected by the Great Depression, may have learned to value money more than their younger counterparts. The decreasing propensity to spend with age may also be the result of their inclination to save, either because they want to maintain their economic independence or due to their experiences during the Great Depression years, or even because they want to leave a legacy (Lazer and Shaw 1987).

The mature consumer's higher propensity to spend and greater propensity to save than their younger counterparts are also confirmed by the results of two studies. One study by *Money* magazine (1987) found that 47 percent of adults 65 and over said they enjoy spending money. Another study by Grey Advertising found one group of older adults liked to save and another enjoyed spending their money (Sharkey 1988).

PREFERENCES FOR METHODS OF PAYMENT

The question of method of payment preferred by older adults is an interesting one and has been addressed in several studies. Yet, most of the results of these studies are descriptive and offer few clues as to the payment methods used or preferred by older shoppers. Let's review the findings of these studies with respect to the most popular methods of payment: credit, cash, and other methods.

Credit

The commonly held view among researchers and practitioners is that older people exhibit low use of credit. This view is supported by data from several studies. One survey of Atlanta residents found only one senior citizen in six (16.6%) to possess a store credit card (Bernhardt and Kinnear 1976). The same study found less than one-quarter of the elderly population to own a gasoline card, compared with 37 to 48 percent of younger groups of respondents. However, the study considered "seniors" to be adults 65 and older. When the analysis was carried out on individuals 50 to 64 years of age, 38.4 percent of them were found to possess store credit cards. In another study, J. Barry Mason and William O. Bearden (1980) examined attitudes toward credit of 100 individuals age 65 and older. While many of them exhibited unfavorable orientation toward credit in general, their responses were not compared to those of younger adults to determine relative preference for credit.

For several reasons, these data appear to provide neither a pattern nor explanations for the observed age-related differences in attitudes and behavior. First, age-related behaviors addressed in regard to credit do not differentiate between ownership of credit cards versus use of credit cards, and the assumption is implicitly made that ownership equals use. This assumption may not hold. For example, according to an American Association for Retired Persons (AARP 1990a) study, while 74 percent of people under 65 years of age (in comparison to 63 percent of those 65 and over) are likely to own at least one or more credit cards, the age difference in use is smaller, with 46 percent of those under 65 and 40 percent of those 65 and over reporting credit card usage more than once a month. Second, studies do not account for different patterns of consumption among the aging population. For example, lower credit use among the elderly might be due to decreased consumption in areas where credit is likely to be used, or decreased frequency of shopping, rather than decreased use of credit in relation to other forms of payment. In fact, the AARP study shows a nearly 30 percent drop in major purchases (those over $300) made after age 65. In fact, when the AARP data were further analyzed by the author and his associates at the Center for Mature Consumer Studies (CMCS), it was found that among those people who go to the store at least once a week to buy products or services (other than food and drug items), older people are as likely as younger adults to use credit as a form of payment. Third, declining use of credit among the 65 and over population might reflect changes in lifestyle and the conditions that "force" one to use more credit in earlier life. For example, an employed person might prefer the use of credit due to safe documentation of expenses for business and tax purposes, something which might not be of concern after retirement. Finally, use of credit is confined to the use of credit cards. It is possible that such credit is substituted for other forms of credit (perhaps of lower cost) available to older adults. For example, one study reported by H. N. Tongren (1988) found that although relatively few older respondents had credit cards, many relied on short-term credit, suggesting that small local retailers may provide credit to their elderly customers whom they have known well over the years.

With respect to differences in attitudes toward credit in general, any observed differences might reflect different values existing among various cohorts, with those who were affected by the Great Depression being the least likely to favor use of credit. It is also possible that the younger generations have been socialized into (i.e., they have learned to like) the use of credit during their development as consumers in early life (Moschis 1987). Such orientations, once developed, tend to persist well into adulthood and become part of the person's personality and lifestyle. Both of these explanations suggest higher credit utilization in late life among future cohorts.

Cash and Other Methods

Other forms of payment include cash, check, and preauthorized service. The use of these methods appears to depend upon the specific type of purchase. For example, Jo-Ann Zbytniewski (1979) found high use of cash among food shoppers age 65 and older, with 98 percent of them indicating this method of payment, compared with 87 percent of those under 65. However, these findings are of limited generalization because they apply to only one type of purchase.

A national study of preferences for payment methods offers additional insights into the various forms preferred (Stanley, Sewall, and Moschis 1982). The study was based on telephone interviews of 1,800 adults selected on the probability basis and compared payment methods used by individuals age 50 and older ($n = 727$) to those used by younger age groups. Respondents were classified according to their preferred method of paying for products and services in 10 major areas, ranging from buying groceries to airline tickets. The payment methods studied ranged from cash and check to various forms of cards and travelers' checks—11 different methods in total. Based on the preferences for the various methods in each purchase situation, respondents were grouped into 5 major categories: cash only (those preferring nothing but cash payment in all purchase situations) (14%), mostly cash (27%), mostly check (17%), bank credit card (10%), and multiple methods (30%). In comparing respondents 50 years of age or older to younger adults, a relatively larger portion of the former group were found in the "cash only" and "multiple method" clusters. In contrast, the "check" and "bank credit card" clusters contained a disproportionately larger number of respondents under 35 years of age.

Finally, use of preauthorized-payment service is a function of need. For example, for products or services consumers must always pay for at any stage in their life cycle (e.g., utilities), use of preauthorized service increases with age, with older people (65+) being at least twice as likely as any other age group to use this service to pay their utility bills. On the other hand, for products and services such as home mortgage and insurance for which ownership or use is not as likely in late life, use of preauthorized-payment service is also likely to be relatively low (Payment Systems, Inc. 1982).

The findings of this study, taken together with those of previous studies, appear to suggest that: (1) preference for a particular payment method may be situation (purchase) specific; (2) different patterns of payment preferences may emerge depending upon the age groups (categories) compared; and (3) preference for payment methods is not uniform within a given age bracket—for example, some groups of older consumers might

Table 5.1
Orientations Toward Saving, Spending, and Use of Payment Systems

	Strongly/ Somewhat Disagree %	Neither Agree Nor Disagree %	Strongly/ Somewhat Agree %
I have a hard time sticking to a savings plan	61.7	16.7	21.7
It is better to save even if you have to do without a few things	5.6	10.7	83.7
I use much of the money I earn/have for personal enjoyment	57.5	21.9	20.5
I enjoy spending money more than I enjoy saving it	43.6	28.5	27.8
I buy many things with a credit card or charge card	48.7	10.0	41.4
As long as people can immediately buy things on credit there is no sense in trying to save for them	74.9	10.0	15.1
I seldom pay off the entire balance on monthly statements of my charge accounts	79.7	4.5	15.8
I like to pay cash for most things I buy	12.2	9.6	78.3
Stores should charge less when a person pays "cash" for products or services	13.7	20.5	65.7
Most stores do not have enough "cash only" registers	17.0	29.8	53.3

Note: Row percentage figures may not add up to 100.0 due to rounding off.

prefer cash or credit, while other groups might have no preference for either method.

NEW INSIGHTS

Our national study sought to offer additional insights into the consumption and financial practices of older Americans—that is, saving, spending, and use of credit and how these practices vary by selected characteristics. Table 5.1 shows responses of the 55-and-over group.

Generally, older adults show positive orientations toward saving. About 60 percent disagree that they have a hard time sticking to a savings plan, and 84 percent agree that it is better to save even if one has to do without a few things. Although older people are likely to keep money aside and they are not likely to spend it to indulge themselves, only one in five indicate that they use much of the money they earn/have for personal enjoyment, and 58 percent disagree, suggesting a conservative spending lifestyle. This is further confirmed by responses older adults give to the statement "I enjoy spending money more than I enjoy saving it," with only slightly over one in four agreeing and 44 percent disagreeing. These findings are consistent with findings of previous studies.

Orientations toward credit use were assessed by asking respondents to indicate their level of agreement or disagreement with two statements. Nearly as many mature adults indicate heavy use of credit as did those who indicate light or no use. However, three-fourths of them say they would rather save for something they want to buy rather than use credit. Collectively, these responses suggest that use of credit is for convenience rather than for financing a higher standard of living. This is also suggested by the large percentage (nearly 80 percent) of the older respondents who disagree with the statement "I seldom pay off the entire balance on monthly statements of my charge accounts."

Although older adults use credit frequently, they prefer paying cash for most of their purchases. Seventy-eight percent appear to prefer cash, as indicated by their response to the statement "I like to pay cash for most things I buy." Because they tend to pay cash, they also feel that stores should provide them with cash discounts, with about two-thirds of them indicating preference for such discounts. Similarly, more than half think that most stores do not have enough "cash only" registers, again suggesting strong preference for cash or convenience, since it usually takes less time to go through "cash only" lines than through regular checkout registers.

Consumer Behavior of Older versus Younger Adults

Responses to finance-related areas provide more useful information when compared to responses given by younger adults. For this reason, answers given by the 55-plus group were compared to responses given by those under 55 years of age. These are shown in Table 5.2. The table shows that younger people, when compared to their older counterparts, have a harder time sticking to a savings plan, and they are somewhat more inclined to indicate a tendency to spend rather than to save. Nearly twice as many younger adults as older express enjoyment in spending rather than saving. This difference may be due to cohort effects. With the older group having lived through the Great Depression, it is expected that their financial habits were influenced by such experience. Alternatively, older adults may hold on to their money more than younger adults who have more years ahead of them during which to take financial risks.

Despite conventional wisdom that older adults use credit less than younger people, our study does not seem to support this belief. Both groups seem to use credit about the same, as indicated by the "agree"

Table 5.2
Orientations Toward Saving, Spending, and Use of Payment Systems among Younger (under 55) and Older (55+) Adults (percentage "strongly/somewhat agree")

	Younger	Older
I have a hard time sticking to a savings plan	37.4	22.1
It is better to save even if you have to do without a few things	76.6	83.3
I use much of the money I earn/have for personal enjoyment	27.3	20.4
I enjoy spending money more than I enjoy saving it	51.3	28.4
I buy many things with a credit card or charge card	40.0	41.8
As long as people can immediately buy things on credit there is no sense in trying to save for them	15.5	14.8
I seldom pay off the entire balance on monthly statements of my charge accounts	28.8	15.3
I like to pay cash for most things I buy	70.4	76.8
Stores should charge less when a person pays "cash" for products or services	50.4	65.2
Most stores do not have enough "cash only" registers	41.5	52.8

responses given to the statement "I buy many things with a credit or charge card." Nor do they seem to differ in their opinion about making an immediate use of credit in comparison to saving for something they want. However, they do appear to differ with regard to the payments they make on credit cards, with nearly twice as many younger adults as older people admitting infrequent payment of the entire balance on monthly statements of their charge accounts. These results, along with preferences for cash among younger versus older adults, suggest that younger people tend to use credit to finance consumption. Preference for cash tends to be lower for people under 55 years of age than among those in the older group. This is also shown in the orientations of the two groups toward cash-related benefits. Specifically, younger adults are not as concerned with getting cash discounts as older adults, nor do they find as many stores having an inadequate number of "cash only" registers.

Sociodemographic Differences

To gain deeper insights into the responses of older people, answers to consumption and finance-related questions were analyzed by selected so-

Table 5.3
Orientations Toward Saving, Spending, and Use of Payment Systems by Age
(percentage "strongly/somewhat agree")

	55-64	65-74	75+
I have a hard time sticking to a savings plan	25.14	13.50	32.02
It is better to save even if you have to do without a few things	81.24	85.25	84.39
I use much of the money I earn/have for personal enjoyment	17.42	23.33	23.65
I enjoy spending money more than I enjoy saving it	31.95	23.31	21.74
I buy many things with a credit card or charge card	40.62	39.80	44.20
As long as people can immediately buy things on credit there is no sense in trying to save for them	16.47	11.90	19.63
I seldom pay off the entire balance on monthly statements of my charge accounts	17.37	13.53	14.89
I like to pay cash for most things I buy	73.67	81.21	84.05
Stores should charge less when a person pays "cash" for products or services	60.23	72.06	65.86
Most stores do not have enough "cash only" registers	55.36	61.19	68.44

ciodemographic characteristics. Table 5.3 shows results broken down by three age groups: 55–64, 65–74, and 75 and over.

As the information in Table 5.3 indicates, ability to save is mostly a concern among the young-old and the very-old mature adults. Also, with age, people find less enjoyment in spending versus saving money. There is also a tendency to prefer paying cash for purchases as well as to appreciate the availability of "cash only" registers in stores.

Because age is a factor associated with many other factors, such as income, sex, marital status, and the like, it was felt that the presence of such factors would contaminate the true effects of age. For example, answers that appear to be related to age among those 75 and over may represent answers due to sex, since women outnumber men by a ratio of two-to-one and tend to be overrepresented in older age groups. To account for such a possibility, the effects of other characteristics that were suspected to show up as "age effects" were removed. This analysis suggests that, with age, mature adults tend to be less likely to have difficulty in developing and following a savings plan; and they are less likely to enjoy spending money and are more likely to enjoy saving it. The latter finding is particularly strong among older Americans in lower income brackets. Similarly, older adults tend to be less likely to favor use of credit for immediate gratification. Rather, they save over a longer time in order to purchase products, and they are more likely to pay off the entire balance of their charge accounts. The latter finding applies only to those in middle and upper income brackets. For the remaining responses, age increasingly contributes to the inclination to agree with all the statements, with the exception of the last statement (see Table 5.3) where preference for "cash only" registers increases with age only among older adults in the middle income bracket.

Financial and consumption practices of older adults are affected by changes in lifestyles associated with age. For example, in comparison to older adults who are employed, unemployed or retired adults have an increasingly harder time sticking to a savings plan. Similarly, the use of money for personal enjoyment drops markedly after the age of 55 among those who are retired but remains relatively unchanged among those who remain employed. Also, the propensity to buy on credit is influenced by work status, with those still employed maintaining a relatively unchanged rate of credit use with age, while use of credit tends to decline with age after retirement. Thus, use of credit may serve other purposes, such as providing documentation of expenses for business or tax purposes.

Responses to the same statements were analyzed according to the older person's sex. Table 5.4 shows the percentage of agreement responses to each statement among male and female older adults. Some of the significant differences in responses deserve mentioning. With respect to attitudes toward saving, there are few differences in responses except when it comes to spending money for personal enjoyment, where males show a stronger tendency to do so than their female counterparts. Males also tend to buy more things on credit than females. Males are also more likely to be of the opinion that stores should give shoppers cash discounts, although they buy more on credit than their female counterparts; and they are more likely to be of the opinion that stores do not have enough "cash only" registers.

Older adults' responses were also analyzed by geographic region. Zip codes were used to classify respondents into four geographic areas. Based on the first 3 digits of the respondent's zip code of his or her permanent residence, the following groupings were developed: east (001–189), south (190–429), north (430–589, 600–699), and west (all remaining). The sample distribution for these four areas was 157, 349, 263, and 159, respectively. Responses given to consumption- and finance-related statements were analyzed by these 4 geographic regions. The results of this analysis are shown in Table 5.5. The analysis applies only to the 55-and-over sample. Some of the geographic differences that emerge are worth noting.

Older adults residing in northern states appear to have a harder time sticking to a savings plan than mature people in other regions. This may be due to their greater inclination to spend a large portion of their avail-

Table 5.4
Orientations Toward Saving, Spending, and Use of Payment Systems by Sex (percentage "strongly/somewhat agree")

	Male	Female
I have a hard time sticking to a savings plan	21.87	20.54
It is better to save even if you have to do without a few things	82.11	83.72
I use much of the money I earn/have for personal enjoyment	25.23	17.05
I enjoy spending money more than I enjoy saving it	25.23	28.68
I buy many things with a credit card or charge card	43.88	37.98
As long as people can immediately buy things on credit there is no sense in trying to save for them	12.69	16.67
I seldom pay off the entire balance on monthly statements of my charge accounts	14.83	16.28
I like to pay cash for most things I buy	79.20	77.13
Stores should charge less when a person pays "cash" for products or services	70.34	62.02
Most stores do not have enough "cash only" registers	56.57	50.78

able income on personal enjoyment. Easterners, in particular, are much more likely to spend on personal enjoyment than, for example, their northerner counterparts. Mature adults living in eastern states are also more likely to buy more things on credit than older people in northern states, while those living in western states tend to be more likely to pay off the entire balance on monthly statements of their charge accounts than their southern counterparts. Finally, with respect to preferences for paying cash and other cash-related benefits, westerners are more likely than those living in eastern states to report preference for cash. Yet, the latter group appears to demand more cash-related benefits. For example, people in eastern states report stronger preferences for cash discounts than older adults in southern states. Similarly, nearly six in ten easterners report a preference for stores with "cash only" registers, compared with only half of mature adults who live in northern or western states.

Household income was also used as a criterion for classifying the responses older respondents in our national study gave to the same statements. Table 5.6 shows responses by three levels of household income: under $30,000; $30,000–$49,999; and $50,000 or more. As expected, ability to put money aside depends partly upon one's available income, with those

Table 5.5
Orientations Toward Saving, Spending, and Use of Payment Systems by Geographic Region (percentage "strongly/somewhat agree")

	East	North	South	West
I have a hard time sticking to a savings plan	21.29	23.44	21.47	16.85
It is better to save even if you have to do without a few things	83.39	84.17	81.30	83.51
I use much of the money I earn/have for personal enjoyment	26.19	16.22	22.20	21.36
I enjoy spending money more than I enjoy saving it	20.34	33.90	28.89	16.87
I buy many things with a credit card or charge card	46.86	35.77	43.11	42.22
As long as people can immediately buy things on credit, there is no sense in trying to save for them	16.03	13.90	16.66	12.33
I seldom pay off the entire balance on my monthly statements of my charge accounts	15.82	15.92	18.11	10.29
I like to pay cash for most things I buy	73.10	77.91	77.39	82.09
Stores should charge less when a person pays "cash" for products or services	72.75	63.95	61.19	67.79
Most stores do not have enough "cash only" registers	58.12	49.92	55.15	50.24
BASE: N = 928	N=157	N=349	N=263	N=159

with less money being less likely to do so. For example, while 23 percent of the older respondents in the under-$30,000 group express difficulty with keeping a savings plan, only 15 percent of those in the $50,000-plus income bracket express such a concern. Similarly, older people's ability to use much of the money they have for personal enjoyment depends upon their level of income, with about 18 percent of those in the under-$50,000 income bracket agreeing with this statement in comparison with 29 percent among those older adults with annual incomes in excess of $50,000. Thus, while enjoyment in spending vis-à-vis saving money is stable with income, ability to do so for personal enjoyment appears to be constrained by income availability.

When it comes to using various types of payment systems, however, mere presence of income does not suggest higher use of cash. On the contrary, use of credit is higher among those mature adults with household

Table 5.6
Orientations Toward Saving, Spending, and Use of Payment Systems by Income (percentage "strongly/somewhat agree")

	Under $30,000	$30,000-49,999	$50,000 or more
I have a hard time sticking to a savings plan	22.87	22.92	14.60
It is better to save even if you have to do without a few things	82.06	82.22	87.55
I use much of the money I earn/have for personal enjoyment	18.62	18.05	28.67
I enjoy spending money more than I enjoy saving it	28.52	25.61	27.72
I buy many things with a credit card or charge card	34.37	40.83	58.56
As long as people can immediately buy things on credit there is no sense in trying to save for them	18.20	11.56	10.87
I seldom pay off the entire balance on monthly statements of my charge accounts	17.67	13.79	12.38
I like to pay cash for most things I buy	83.18	72.83	69.11
Stores should charge less when a person pays "cash" for products or services	64.78	71.22	58.31
Most stores do not have enough "cash only" registers	53.75	55.10	47.94

incomes in excess of $50,000 than among those in the lower income brackets. There is also some evidence of deferred gratification among higher-income older adults, although they can easily afford purchases, in comparison to those with less money. Nearly twice as many of those with incomes less than $30,000 agree that as long as people can immediately buy things on credit there is no sense in trying to save for them, in comparison to those whose household income exceeds $50,000.

With income, there appears to be a steady decline in preferences for paying cash. A larger percentage in the middle income group than their higher income counterparts demand cash discounts. Similar differences are found with respect to preference for "cash only" registers among the two groups.

Lifestyles and Consumer Behavior

Four need-based groups were formed (see Appendix F), reflecting four different lifestyles; these were also used to explain differences in responses

Table 5.7
Orientations Toward Saving, Spending, and Use of Payment Systems by Need-Based Clusters (percentage "strongly/somewhat agree")

	Self-Sufficients	Young Insecureds	Dependent Frail	Struggling Full-Nesters
I have a hard time sticking to a savings plan	19.57	23.24	19.03	34.15
It is better to save even if you have to do without a few things	81.77	82.70	82.46	85.37
I use much of the money I earn/have for personal enjoyment	26.54	21.08	23.88	12.20
I enjoy spending money more than I enjoy saving it	24.66	30.37	26.87	28.46
I buy many things with a credit card or charge card	41.02	40.54	45.90	43.90
As long as people can immediately buy things on credit, there is no sense in trying to save for them	12.06	11.89	14.93	19.51
I seldom pay off the entire balance on my monthly statements of my charge accounts	13.61	18.92	11.94	20.33
I like to pay cash for most things I buy	79.36	75.68	78.73	77.24
Stores should charge less when a person pays "cash" for products or services	67.83	65.41	69.40	68.29
Most stores do not have enough "cash only" registers	56.30	58.38	51.12	52.03

to consumption- and finance-related statements. Table 5.7 shows agreement responses of each of the four groups.

The group most likely to have a hard time sticking to a savings plan is the struggling full-nesters, with 34 percent of older adults in this group expressing this orientation. On the other hand, the dependent frail group is the least likely to do so, with fewer than one in five expressing this attitude. Also, in comparison to the remaining groups, struggling full-nesters are less likely to use their savings to indulge themselves, with 12 percent of them expressing this inclination, in comparison with 27 percent of self-sufficients, 21 percent of young insecureds, and 24 percent of dependent frail. Attitudes toward immediate gratification via use of credit, however, are stronger among the struggling full-nesters than among the self-sufficients and young insecureds. Nearly one in five of the former group, in comparison with about 12 percent of each of the later groups,

Table 5.8
Orientations Toward Savings, Spending, and Use of Payment Systems by Gerontographic Clusters (percentage "strongly/somewhat agree")

	Healthy Hermits	Ailing Outgoers	Frail Recluses	Healthy Indulgers
I have a hard time sticking to a savings plan	65.21	54.66	58.78	54.33
It is better to save even if you have to do without a few things	80.82	81.67	81.76	91.34
I use much of the money I earn/have for personal enjoyment	23.01	24.13	22.30	19.69
I buy many things with a credit card or charge card	46.30	37.30	40.54	48.03
As long as people can immediately buy things on credit, there is no sense in trying to save for them	11.23	17.04	16.22	10.24
I seldom pay off the entire balance on my monthly statements of my charge accounts	9.04	21.22	14.86	18.11
I like to pay cash for most things I buy	74.25	85.85	78.38	69.29
Stores should charge less when a person pays "cash" for products or services	66.58	71.38	69.59	61.42
Most stores do not have enough "cash only" registers	50.14	57.88	59.35	55.12

agrees that as long as people can immediately buy things on credit there is no sense in trying to save for them. Similarly, the struggling full-nesters and the young insecureds are less likely to pay off the entire balance of their charge accounts than the dependent frail. Finally, a larger percentage of young insecureds are likely to demand more "cash only" registers than their counterparts labeled as "dependent frail."

Consumer Behavior of Gerontographic Segments

Finally, responses to consumption- and finance-related statements were examined among gerontographic segments. The results of this analysis are shown in Table 5.8. Healthy hermits are more likely than ailing outgoers and healthy indulgers to indicate difficulty with sticking to a savings plan. Healthy indulgers, on the other hand, are more likely to emphasize savings over consumption than any of the remaining groups. This appears to be the case in spite of the fact that a larger percentage of the healthy indulgers are more inclined to buy things on credit, in comparison with, for example, ailing outgoers or frail recluses. Obviously, high credit usage among healthy indulgers is due to convenience, not due to attitude toward credit as a means of financing a higher standard of living. This was attested to by further analysis of the data, which revealed that older adults who tend to buy things on credit are usually those who are the *least* likely to favor immediate gratification via use of credit.

Although ailing outgoers are less likely to use credit to buy products and services, they are the group least likely to pay off the entire balance of their monthly statements of their charge accounts, in comparison with healthy hermits. Ailing outgoers prefer paying cash in comparison with healthy hermits and healthy indulgers. Orientations toward cash-related benefits are also higher among ailing outgoers and, to a lesser extent, among frail recluses in comparison with healthy indulgers. Similarly, a larger percentage of frail recluses and ailing outgoers prefer more "cash only" checkout registers than healthy hermits.

SUMMARY AND IMPLICATIONS

To summarize the consumption and financial behavior of older Americans, today's mature consumer does not appear to fit the stereotype of an older person. Older adults hold on to their money and do not enjoy spending it, and the more money they have, the more they enjoy saving than spending it. Credit is widely used among older Americans; however, credit is used more for convenience than as a means of financing a higher standard of living. Use of credit does not necessarily mean carrying more cards, but rather a higher frequency of paying by credit card when it is convenient to do so. In contrast, younger consumers must use credit to finance purchases, and they often must use it even if it is not convenient to do so. Credit use appears to be determined by changes in lifestyles and social situations that are associated with age, rather than by age per se. Thus, the challenge for marketers is not so much in developing products and services that older people can afford. Rather, successful marketing solutions lie more in the ability to change older consumers' attitudes toward spending and in giving reasons for and enjoyment in spending money. Credit should be positioned primarily as a convenience-enhancing service rather than as a vehicle for financing purchases.

6

Preferences for Sources of Information

Information seeking is an important aspect of consumer behavior in general. Information determines which products and brands consumers will consider and how they are likely to perceive these offerings. Thus, understanding how consumers gather and use information helps marketers determine the types of information consumers need and the sources through which such information should be made available to them.

This chapter addresses two issues: (1) What sources of consumer information do older people rely on most in making various types of purchasing decisions? (2) How can businesses better promote to, or inform, older consumers about new products and services? Because information-source utilization is likely to vary by type of consumer decision and over the life cycle, the main issues are addressed by type of product and service and by age group. Previous research is first summarized, and in turn the results of our national survey are presented to expand on existing knowledge and offer additional insights into the questions raised.

PATTERNS OF INFORMATION USE

A person's use of, and reliance upon, a particular source of information is likely to change over his or her life cycle. A national study conducted by Market Facts, Inc., for the American Association of Retired Persons (AARP 1990a) found that with increasing age people tend to use fewer sources of information in making major purchases (those over $300). Similarly, Mary C. Gilly and Valarie A. Zeithaml (1985) found that the elderly use information sources differently than the nonelderly to learn about in-

Table 6.1
Sources of Information for Travel and Entertainment by Age

	Under 45	45-54	55-64	65-74	75+
Son(s)/Daughter(s)	26.27	48.33	45.87	43.20	35.65
Spouse	42.21	56.44	45.90	34.01	31.15
Mother/Father	37.32	10.43	3.33	2.50	1.53
Radio & TV Ads/Programs	69.11	58.60	61.85	48.32	57.76
Newspapers/Magazines	55.44	60.16	57.77	55.63	48.20
Business Owners/Employees	23.15	20.47	9.32	4.62	1.53
Friends/Acquaintances	67.55	71.34	68.65	64.47	60.29

Note: Table entries are percentages of those in each age category aware of information through the specific source.

novations. Thus, older people may use and rely on various sources of consumer information differently than younger people.

Past buying experience is the source of information most often utilized not just by older adults but by younger adults as well. In fact, the AARP study (1990a) found that past buying experience was more likely to be used by younger than by older adults in making major purchases. The same was the case with all other sources of information examined, including articles or books about products or services and product ratings from consumer magazines. However, most of the available research points to greater use of, and reliance on, formal sources of consumer information with increasing age in late life. This tendency may be the result of voluntary or involuntary withdrawal from life and from previously established personal contacts. As older adults are likely to experience a "constriction of life space" (or a reduction in the variety of interpersonal sources), they may increasingly rely on mass media (television and newspapers, in particular) to compensate for their previously established behaviors. Thus, it is not surprising to find most of the relevant published data in support of this line of reasoning showing a much greater reliance on commercial sources by older than by younger consumers (Moschis 1992b). The inconsistency with the findings of the AARP survey may be due to possible confounding effects of frequency of major purchases on frequency of source utilization, and because this study questioned respondents only about important purchases (in excess of $300) while other studies did not specify the nature of the purchase. Personal sources are likely to be used to the extent that these are available and accessible to the older shopper, and the product is important enough to stimulate informal communication. The product-importance requirement for word-of-mouth communication is also supported by the AARP study, which showed family or friends' advice to be most important among the 85-and-over age group.

Our national survey investigated a number of different sources of information for a wide variety of products and services. Specifically, the sources of information examined were: son(s)/daughter(s), spouse, mother/father, radio and TV ads/programs, newspapers and magazines, business owners and employees, and friends/acquaintances. The purchase situations were: travel and entertainment, financial matters, grocery products, clothes and fashion, appliances and furniture, medical and health-care services, new products and services, home-related matters, and shopping and sales in general. Respondents were asked to indicate the source(s) of information that help them become aware of new products and services in each of the nine categories mentioned. Responses to information sources for each of the categories were broken down by age groups—under 45, 45–54, 55–64, 65–74, and 75 and over.

TRAVEL AND ENTERTAINMENT

There is relatively little published research on information sources older adults use in making various types of leisure decisions. Previous research found that travel agents are a significant source concerning travel decisions (Moschis 1992b). In our research, we asked respondents to tell us how they become informed about travel and entertainment services. Responses to various sources of information were classified by age categories. Table 6.1 shows responses to these sources of information for travel and entertainment among the various age groups.

With respect to the relative importance of the various information sources, the data in Table 6.1 show that peers and acquaintances are a very important source of information regarding travel and entertainment. Mass media sources are also very important in making older people aware of the availability of new travel and entertainment services. With respect to the importance of the various sources over the person's lifespan, the older person's children are most useful as a source of information in mid-life. Perhaps the presence of children in the household enhances their importance as an information source. A somewhat similar pattern exists for the person's spouse as a source of information, reflecting presence/absence of spouse in the household during various stages of life. The significance of the older person's parents as information sources decreases with age. This reflects the aging person's perception of his or her parent's ability to provide useful information as well as a higher incidence of deceased parents. The importance of peers is significant and remains relatively strong over the person's life cycle. Because of shrinking social networks with increasing age, the older person may place an increasingly greater value on the opinion of available peers.

Use of commercial sources of information also varies with age. The importance of print media remains high over the person's life cycle. Utilizing radio and TV ads and programs as sources of information is highest among the youngest age group and lowest among those in the 65-to-74 bracket. With age, the influence of business owners or employees (e.g., travel agents) declines as a useful information source.

FINANCIAL MATTERS

The national study of intergenerational consumer perceptions conducted by the Center for Mature Consumer Studies (CMCS) (Moschis et al. 1991) asked older adults to indicate the sources they consider helpful in keeping them informed about financial services. Respondents cited newspaper or magazine ads as the most helpful, with more than one-third of them (34.9%) citing these print media. Advocate sources were a distant second (27.1%), followed by salespeople and other professionals (22.6%), direct mail (21.6%), and radio and TV ads (20.4%). Social sources were the least helpful. A total of 16.2 percent cited spouse, and a smaller percentage cited friends/acquaintances/neighbors (12.1%), their children (8.3%), and other relatives (7.4%). However, in choosing financial institutions, another study found personal sources to be significantly more important to approximately 300 older adults (age 45 and older) than the marketer-dominated sources of print and broadcast advertising and sales contacts made with the potential customer by the financial institution (Schutz, Baird, and Hawkes 1979). The only marketer-controlled source of information for financial institutions that approached the importance level of personal sources was the yellow pages. Decisions on investments for retirement income were primarily based on personal judgment and experience, with an estimated 38 percent of the respondents surveyed reporting reliance on personal judgment. Family and friends' opinions were used less frequently, with an estimated 26.3 percent reporting reliance on these sources.

For insurance policies, older adults appear to use similar sources to those used in deciding on investments for retirement. In Howard G. Schutz, Pamela C. Baird, and Glenn R. Hawkes's study (1979), for example, nearly half (47.7%) of the older adults surveyed indicated use of personal judgment and experience; family and friends were second (31.9%), followed by professional directories and referral services (9.8%) and consumer publications (5.3%).

Because Schutz, Baird, and Hawkes's study did not analyze age differences of those age 45 and older, our research sought to resolve inconsistencies in previous research findings. Information sources for financial

Table 6.2
Sources of Information for Financial Matters by Age

	Under 45	45-54	55-64	65-74	75+
Son(s)/Daughter(s)	7.76	38.31	37.06	33.11	35.95
Spouse	53.40	66.66	52.92	46.99	37.35
Mother/Father	48.60	21.61	5.86	2.58	0.77
Radio & TV Ads/Programs	45.50	34.10	41.57	37.38	41.78
Newspapers/Magazines	53.20	49.58	54.13	46.09	47.44
Business Owners/Employees	40.69	39.91	20.45	10.83	9.72
Friends/Acquaintances	48.62	52.05	38.71	33.96	40.78

Note: Table entries are percentages of those in each age category aware of information through the specific source.

matters according to age groups are shown in Table 6.2. The table shows that significant sources of consumer information include spouse, friends/acquaintances, mass media, and, to a lesser extent, one's children. These results are not quite consistent with those of previous studies. For example, while the CMCS study found spouse, children, and peers to play only a minor role in helping older adults keep informed of new developments in the area of financial services, our study found these sources to play a more important role. Perhaps these differences may be attributed to the way the two studies asked the same questions. While the CMCS study questioned respondents on "financial services," our study asked respondents to indicate their opinion on sources of information on "financial matters."

One's adult children are an important source of information about financial matters over that person's life cycle. The importance of one's spouse as a source of financial information declines somewhat with age, reflecting the increasing number of older adults without a spouse in late life. Similarly, the importance of peers appears to decline with age, reflecting the older person's increasing isolation or withdrawal.

Use of print media as a source of financial information remains relatively stable over the person's life cycle, and the same appears to be the case for broadcast media. With increasing age, older adults tend to rely less on retail vendors and personnel for information about new financial services. Thus, both mass media and personal sources of information appear to be important, but their importance tends to vary over the person's life span.

Table 6.3
Sources of Information for Grocery Products by Age

	Under 45	45-54	55-64	65-74	75+
Son(s)/Daughter(s)	15.67	31.91	25.56	23.74	21.57
Spouse	35.07	37.99	47.98	41.33	37.81
Mother/Father	37.62	21.30	6.37	2.96	3.06
Radio & TV Ads/Programs	63.74	61.33	54.91	48.20	36.65
Newspapers/Magazines	63.71	67.55	66.05	59.12	56.92
Business Owners/Employees	7.30	11.48	3.94	1.15	3.60
Friends/Acquaintances	37.88	47.07	36.18	37.11	43.98

Note: Table entries are percentages of those in each age category aware of information through the specific source.

GROCERY PRODUCTS

Food products are less significant to the older consumer than other purchases, at least from an economic viewpoint, and do not justify as much expenditure of energy to seek out information. As a result, most of the information gathering comes either from the most convenient source—that is, the person's own memory or in-store sources. One study (Moschis 1992b), for example, found that 52.3 percent of older respondents reported using their own judgment in deciding on frozen vegetables, and another 20.5 percent used package labels. Family and friends were a distant third (11.4%), followed by displays and samples (6.3%). In studying five food products, the National Food Processors Association (1990) found that older consumers (age 50 and older) more than other age groups want information provided on product packages. This desire for more information is also related to the existence of dietary restrictions (such as reduced sodium or cholesterol intake). It appears that with age older people develop dietary or other health-related concerns that increase their propensity to examine the ingredients of food products.

Our survey also investigated sources of information for grocery products. The intent of this study was to supplement existing findings, focusing on the role of mass media and other personal sources not previously examined. Table 6.3 shows use of information sources for grocery products by age group. As the table shows, newspapers and magazines are very important sources of information regarding new grocery products. Of

Table 6.4
Sources of Information for Clothes and Fashion by Age

	Under 45	45-54	55-64	65-74	75+
Son(s)/Daughter(s)	32.49	56.36	45.61	30.51	17.98
Spouse	31.78	33.44	36.69	27.68	32.68
Mother/Father	18.12	10.20	1.60	2.19	0.77
Radio & TV Ads/Programs	58.73	53.79	50.88	42.89	36.12
Newspapers/Magazines	72.59	66.00	63.69	66.96	53.86
Business Owners/Employees	10.99	15.31	5.97	3.48	1.53
Friends/Acquaintances	56.26	47.57	41.47	35.78	37.79

Note: Table entries are percentages of those in each age category aware of information through the specific source.

nearly equal importance are radio and TV advertisements and programs. Spouse, friends, and acquaintances are the most important personal sources of information regarding grocery products. The importance of most of these sources depends a lot on the person's stage in life. The influence of one's children gradually declines with age, while the influence of spouse is highest among consumers age 55 to 64. The importance of peers remains fairly stable over the person's life cycle, as does the importance of print media. The importance of broadcast media, on the other hand, declines with age.

CLOTHES AND FASHION

When buying clothing items, older adults place more emphasis on informal sources of information (family, friends) than on salespeople and ads. This does not come as a surprise, since the purchase of clothes involves a certain level of social risk that consumers must reduce before making a decision. It is logical, therefore, that social (informal) sources would be consulted to reduce such a risk.

Table 6.4 shows classification of information-source-utilization responses by age group. Print media are by far the most important sources of consumer information regarding clothes and fashion. Broadcast media play a secondary, yet important, role, while friends/acquaintances and one's children are the most important personal sources of information about clothes and fashion. The importance of children's influence appears to decline sharply with advancing age in late life, while the influence of spouse remains rather constant. Peer influence also declines. The effects of broadcast media appear to decline beginning early in life, while the print media continue to be important sources of consumer information well into late life.

APPLIANCES AND FURNITURE

Mass media play an important role in the purchase of household appliances, according to a national consumer survey sponsored by Whirlpool Corporation and conducted by CMCS (Moschis et al. 1991). While print media sources were identified as most useful (56.0%), word-of-mouth recommendations were still important in keeping older adults informed about home appliances on the market, with four respondents in ten (39.9%) considering at least one personal information source to be helpful. One-quarter (24.9%) identified spouses as helpful sources of information about appliances. Recommendations from friends and neighbors, one's children, and other relatives were reported as somewhat less useful than many commercial sources. Nearly one-fifth (18.5%) named salespeople as helpful sources of information about appliances. More than one-third (35.6%) of the respondents judged brochures or catalogs from the manufacturer of almost equal value with radio and TV ads. While commercial sources are considered to be most important in keeping older consumers informed about appliances, personal judgment and personal sources appear to dominate the decision to buy appliances such as television sets. In Schutz, Baird, and Hawkes's (1979) study, the percentages of those using these two sources for such products were 47.7 percent and 21.7 percent, respectively; interestingly, however, consumer publications were a close third, with 18.1 percent of the mature respondents surveyed expressing preference for this source.

Neither the CMCS study nor Schutz, Baird, and Hawkes's study compared responses between younger and older adults, although respondents in the latter study were age 45 and older. Thus, our national study was aimed at analyzing differences in responses among different age groups. The intent of this study was not only to validate and expand information on this topic but also to analyze the importance of these sources over the person's lifespan.

The results of our national study confirm those of previous studies. Mass media appear to play an important role in helping older adults to keep up with developments in the area of furniture and appliances (Table 6.5). Regardless of one's stage in the lifespan, print and broadcast media are used by at least half of the respondents surveyed. Friends/acquaintances are valued by roughly one-third of older respondents, while one's spouse is considered to be an important source by a little over one-third of these respondents.

With respect to the importance of various information sources over

Table 6.5
Sources of Information for Appliances and Furniture by Age

	Under 45	45-54	55-64	65-74	75+
Son(s)/Daughter(s)	5.59	30.13	27.85	24.01	20.04
Spouse	37.79	44.84	41.95	33.14	31.69
Mother/Father	27.98	10.58	1.16	1.67	1.53
Radio & TV Ads/Programs	60.20	56.33	56.72	53.14	49.73
Newspapers/Magazines	65.94	64.36	66.58	68.18	49.73
Business Owners/Employees	9.56	16.83	8.25	3.81	3.83
Friends/Acquaintances	38.19	36.58	32.46	31.22	33.89

Note: Table entries are percentages of those in each age category aware of information through the specific source.

one's lifespan, the influence of peers tends to persist into late life while spouse's influence tends to decline. Broadcast media sources are important throughout life, while the importance of print media drops sharply after age 75, perhaps reflecting decline in propensity to buy these products in late life.

MEDICAL AND HEALTH-CARE SERVICES

The national study for Whirlpool Corporation conducted by CMCS (Moschis et al. 1991) asked a random sample of 1,275 Americans, including 769 adults age 55 and older, to indicate the helpfulness of various information sources in keeping them informed about health-care products and services in the marketplace. Newspapers and magazine ads were most frequently mentioned by older adults (38.9%), followed by radio and TV ads (30.0%) and advocate sources like *Consumer Reports*, editorial columns, TV programs, and so on (25.9%). Approximately one in five mentioned direct mail (22.3%), spouse (18.9%), friends/acquaintances (18.7%), and salespeople or other professionals (18.5%). Other relatives and one's children were last on the list, with 10.0 and 7.0 percent of the older respondents, respectively, considering these sources to be helpful in keeping them informed about health-care services. In a study by Elaine Sherman and Andrew M. Forman reported in *Maturity Market Report* (1988), personal sources of information ranked higher than mass media for health-care decisions (products and services). Schutz, Baird, and Hawkes's (1979) study examined information source utilization in selecting

Table 6.6
Sources of Information for Medical and Health Care Services by Age

	Under 45	45-54	55-64	65-74	75+
Son(s)/Daughter(s)	5.47	26.91	24.07	28.28	33.59
Spouse	36.88	54.17	51.22	44.03	40.41
Mother/Father	49.87	39.53	13.48	5.41	2.30
Radio & TV Ads/Programs	49.97	43.86	51.31	46.33	45.60
Newspapers/Magazines	38.31	43.18	50.50	53.04	52.33
Business Owners/Employees	27.25	29.15	15.65	6.31	5.89
Friends/Acquaintances	40.65	44.46	48.07	51.87	48.27

Note: Table entries are percentages of those in each age category aware of
information through the specific source.

health-care practitioners and found family and friends to be most important (41.1%) followed by personal experience and judgment (35.0%) and
professional directories and referral services (18.1%). Yellow pages and
newspapers were last, with 3.9 percent and 0.3 percent of older respondents, respectively, showing preference for these sources. In a study conducted by Teresa A. Swartz and Nancy Stephens (1984), personal sources
were found to be significantly more important than yellow pages or doctor
contacts. The authors attributed the difference in the ratings to the more
evaluative value of information available through personal sources. On
the other hand, for cold remedies, pharmacists are the main source of
information, according to another study by R. Michman, R. Hocking, and
L. Harris (1981). Another survey by Robert J. VanDellen (1990) of consumers in 12 major markets found that among people over age 54, 60
percent said they would call a physician in response to a newspaper ad-
vertisement, 47 percent would do the same in response to a radio commercial, and 32 percent in response to a television commercial.

To summarize the results of previous studies, while the studies by CMCS
(Moschis et al. 1991) and VanDellen (1990) highlight the importance of
mass media ads, the remaining studies highlight the importance of personal sources of information. To provide additional insights into these
inconsistent findings, our national study asked respondents to indicate the
extent to which they keep informed of developments in the health-care
field via different sources of information. Table 6.6 shows responses to
various information sources by age group.

While mass media sources are important, personal sources are of equal

Table 6.7
Sources of Information for New Products and Services by Age

	Under 45	45-54	55-64	65-74	75+
Son(s)/Daughter(s)	10.83	32.29	25.92	21.67	18.74
Spouse	22.66	24.83	25.78	18.70	21.97
Mother/Father	17.08	7.01	2.67	0.90	0.00
Radio & TV Ads/Programs	77.65	70.58	69.04	66.16	64.88
Newspapers/Magazines	70.25	70.96	66.67	64.16	54.86
Business Owners/Employees	17.74	22.82	10.37	4.38	2.30
Friends/Acquaintances	45.99	45.49	38.53	36.95	37.79

Note: Table entries are percentages of those in each age category aware of information through the specific source.

importance. About half of older adults age 55 and over report awareness of medical and health-care information through magazines/newspapers and friends/acquaintances. Nearly as many find out about medical and health-related matters from radio or TV ads or programs and their spouses.

Sources of information for health-care services appear to vary in importance over the life cycle. Among personal sources, relatives play an important role, with the influence of one's children increasing and that of spouse decreasing with age. Peer influence tends to remain relatively stable. Interestingly, broadcast media remain an important source of information over the lifespan while the importance of print media actually increases with age. The latter finding may be due to the aging person's increasing sensitivity to health-related topics triggered by his or her failing health.

NEW PRODUCTS AND SERVICES

Besides the product/service-specific questions about sources of information addressed, our study asked broader types of questions regarding three broad areas: new products and services, home-related matters, and shopping and sales.

Table 6.7 shows responses to new products and services with respect to sources of information by age group. Although personal sources are not as important as mass media, peer influence is particularly high and nearly twice as frequent as that of relatives. Mass media sources are particularly

Table 6.8
Sources of Information for Home-Related Matters by Age

	Under 45	45-54	55-64	65-74	75+
Son(s)/Daughter(s)	28.89	54.73	43.83	38.74	41.31
Spouse	63.53	77.48	68.76	57.65	41.17
Mother/Father	50.95	32.41	9.26	2.77	2.30
Radio & TV Ads/Programs	18.68	21.91	20.45	21.32	26.40
Newspapers/Magazines	20.21	29.04	31.74	29.26	24.10
Business Owners/Employees	7.31	9.17	3.87	1.29	2.30
Friends/Acquaintances	43.65	39.00	36.20	32.65	33.66

Note: Table entries are percentages of those in each age category aware of
        information through the specific source.

important, especially radio and TV ads or programs. Sources of information used for new products/services change over the life span. Children's influence declines over the life cycle. The influence of spouse remains fairly stable, regardless of loss of spouse in late life, suggesting that the importance of this source may increase in late life. The influence of various types of mass media declines slightly in late life. Peer influence remains fairly stable in later life despite increasing social isolation.

HOME-RELATED MATTERS

Although personal judgment has been found to be an important determinant of the older adult's decision concerning home care services (Schutz, Baird, and Hawkes 1979), family and friends' recommendations also appear to be more important in deciding, for example, which plumbing company to use. Family and friends are on the top of the list (37.0%), followed by yellow pages (29.1%), personal judgment and experience (24.7%), and professional directories and referral services (7.2%) (Schutz, Baird, and Hawkes 1979).

In our study, as shown in Table 6.8, personal sources of information appear to be of much greater significance than commercial sources. Specifically, the influence of one's children, spouse, and peers is rather high and tends to decline with age. Broadcast media are of lesser importance, and their influence persists into late life. The same appears to be the case with print media whose influence tends to decline in late life.

SHOPPING AND SALES

Both personal and commercial sources of information for shopping and sales play an important role. Peers are particularly important in communicating product information, while the influence of spouse and children tends to decline in late life. Commercial sources of information are also important. Both broadcast and print media influences decline with age, with the print media playing a relatively more important role.

Further analysis was conducted to assess the characteristics of older Americans who are inclined to use mass media and personal sources of information. Mature consumers who use the mass media for consumer information are more likely to be of higher socioeconomic status and female, and they are more likely to live with their spouse or other family members than to live alone. On the other hand, mature consumers who use personal sources of information are likely to be in a higher social class, to be female, and to live with the spouse and/or others. Thus, sources of consumer information may be used as complementary rather than competing sources.

SUMMARY AND IMPLICATIONS

The research findings presented in this chapter suggest that the value of a specific source of information in the older person's consumer decisions is likely to vary by factors such as the type of product or service involved and the older person's stage in life. Furthermore, while older Americans consider commercial sources of information to be important in keeping informed about the marketplace, they tend to rely less on them in making purchasing decisions. However, the relative importance of the mass media and personal sources as sources of awareness and influence also depends on the type of product or service. The more expensive the product or service, the greater the influence of personal sources; the less expensive the product, the greater the influence of mass media.

The implications of these findings for marketers who wish to communicate effectively with the aged population are several. First, it is suggested that marketing sources of information should be used that take into consideration the characteristics of the product or service and target market. Second, communicators should avoid using the same promotional mix for different products and services; rather, promotion needs should be based on the nature of the product or service being marketed. Finally, planners of communication strategies should use various channels of communication in a complementary fashion. Mass media should be used to create awareness, and personal sources should be sought out in an attempt to create word-of-mouth communications, especially for relatively expensive products and services.

PART IV

DEVELOPING MARKETING PROGRAMS

7

Analyzing Orientations Toward Products

Firms interested in targeting the older consumer are faced with a number of decisions regarding the development and marketing of products and services. These range from new product development to minor modifications in product features to better satisfy the needs of older consumers. In the area of product management, product decisions do not necessarily involve new product development and change. Marketers may simply promote the same products differently or position them in a way that would be of greater appeal to the older person. Thus, decisions concerning the development and marketing of products and services range widely in scope. Regardless of the nature of the decision, managers need to understand older persons' needs, attitudes, and perceptions of existing products. Understanding such needs would enable marketers to design products and services to satisfy older consumer needs, modify existing products or services, or even position them differently to better serve the needs of the marketer. Chapter 8 examines the area of new product development and adoption, while this chapter examines older consumers' orientations toward existing products and services. Such orientations range from perceptions of specific product features to satisfaction with existing products and brand loyalty.

DIS/SATISFACTION WITH PRODUCTS AND SERVICES

To summarize the existing evidence of older consumer satisfaction and dissatisfaction, we find that older consumers tend to be more satisfied with products and services than their younger counterparts, but this might be true only for specific products or types of businesses. For products and services that older persons are likely to interact with on a more frequent basis as they age, the level of satisfaction is likely to be lower. This appears to be especially true for products and services whose consumption requires the performance of various activities by the older person, activities likely to be affected by biophysical changes in late life. For such products and services, older persons might attribute poor performance to the product or service provider, since they are likely to adapt to these changes and may not be aware of their own limitations (Moschis 1992b).

While previous research is useful in helping us assess overall satisfaction, little information is available on specific areas of consumer discontent. What are specific areas of older consumer satisfaction or dissatisfaction? Are those older consumers who possess certain characteristics more likely to be dissatisfied or satisfied with specific areas of marketing activities?

In our national study, dissatisfaction was assessed by asking respondents to agree or disagree with five statements addressing negative processes and effects of buying and using products. Table 7.1 shows "agree-disagree" responses to these statements. As the table shows, older consumers are rather dissatisfied with the products and services they buy. Nearly four in five indicated they often wished they could get their money back for products/services purchased. Even a higher percentage of older adults indicated that some things they buy do not work as well as they are supposed to.

Another way of assessing older consumers' discontent is by examining their actions as a result of negative experiences with products and services. Four in five provided affirmative responses to the statement "I make it a point to let others know of products and services I am not happy with."

When it comes to evaluating specific product attributes, older adults are likely to give manufacturers of products low marks. Nearly sixty percent agreed that letters on packages and labels are too small to read. Another 70 percent said that they often find packages and containers very difficult to open.

PRODUCT EVALUATION AND SELECTION

Before we can begin addressing the question of how older adults evaluate products and services, we must keep in mind that product evaluation may not occur as frequently as one might think. Product or service evaluation involves both information seeking and information processing, activities that can be taxing on the older person. For example, consider the following propositions suggested by research on how older people process information (Moschis 1987, p. 197):

The information-processing abilities of the aging consumer undergo significant changes as a result of biological changes common in later stages of the person's

Table 7.1
Orientations Toward Products

	Strongly/ Somewhat Disagree %	Neither Agree Nor Disagree %	Strongly/ Somewhat Agree %
Dissatisfaction with Products and Services			
I sometimes wish I could get my money back for some things I bought	7.0	14.8	78.3
Some things I buy do not work as well as they are supposed to	6.6	10.7	82.7
I make it a point to let others know of products and services I am not happy with	9.6	15.1	75.3
I often find the letters on packages and labels too small to read	25.0	15.4	59.6
I often find packages and containers very difficult to open	14.7	15.5	69.7
Purchase of New Products			
I try to learn as much as I can about a new product/service before buying or using it	5.3	17.6	77.1
I pay little attention to product warranties and guarantees	53.7	12.6	33.8
I often become confused if I have to consider a lot of information about a product I am thinking of buying	31.6	24.7	43.7
I often do not know what to look for in choosing among different brands	41.1	24.8	34.1
Brand Loyalty			
I try to stick to well-known brands	12.3	19.1	68.5
I prefer a certain brand of most products I buy	9.0	19.8	71.3
I like to try something new every time I am in the store	56.3	30.0	13.6

Note: Row percentage figures may not add up to 100.0 due to rounding off.

life. With increasing age, older persons process information less efficiently because they:

(a) need more time to follow stimuli that cross the visual field quickly.

(b) are becoming unable to see and use concrete information, abstract relationships, and patterns.

(c) have a decreasing ability to screen out irrelevant information.

(d) are becoming increasingly unable to differentiate between stimuli.

(e) are becoming less able to recall newly gathered information.

(f) are becoming less able to integrate newly gathered information into a previously established cognitive structure.

While physical search for new information appears to decline with age, the need for product information appears to exist and even to intensify with age among those who are socially isolated (Moschis 1987). J. C. Doolittle (1979) provides evidence that news usage from the mass media is highest among older adults who have the least social interaction. News and information that at one time may have been obtained in the workplace or in other social settings are obtained by older people from the mass media (Kubey 1980).

Declining ability to process information and evaluate products and services may account for the older person's greater susceptibility to persuasive messages and to less than optimal choices. Therefore, reliance on the available information in the person's environment may not always assist the aging person. Thus, it is not surprising that older adults rely more on personal experiences (internal information) than on external stimuli with increasing age.

When older consumers evaluate brands and products or services, they must use a number of *criteria* or *attributes*. These tend to vary across products and services, but we can mention a few that tend to apply to several situations.

Price

Price is always an important consideration in almost any purchasing decision, especially among older consumers. A Food Marketing Institute study, for example, found that older adults look for store specials more than any other age group (Miklos 1982). However, the importance of price as a criterion in decision making tends to vary by type of purchase situation. A study of 715 adults age 55 and older conducted by the Center for Mature Consumer Studies (CMCS) (Moschis 1989) found that price becomes increasingly important as the value or quality of the product or service becomes standardized. When product quality or performance varies, price is likely to play a secondary role. Generally, value is believed to be far more important than price among older adults (*Senior Market Report* 1988).

Guarantees/Warranties

While guarantees and warranties are not salient attributes in every purchase situation, whenever relevant, they are important. One study, for example, found that older consumers demand guarantees and warranties more than the average consumer (Schewe 1985). Similarly, a study by Donnelley Marketing found that people age 50 and older rated unconditional guarantees as the most important influence in causing them to buy, much higher than those age 25 to 49 did (Balkite 1988). Similarly, a study by the Whirlpool Corporation (1983) showed that guarantees become increasingly important with age.

Such an increasing emphasis on guarantees may reflect the older person's desire to reduce risks associated with purchases. The desire to maintain peace of mind is also reflected in older persons' propensity to prefer product samples, buy products "made in America," prefer manufacturers with local service centers, and consider safety to be more important than their younger counterparts (*American Demographics* 1990; Balkite 1988; Whirlpool 1983; Moschis et al. 1991).

While many criteria are almost equally used by younger adults as well (Moschis 1992b), other criteria such as guarantees appear to be of greater value to older than to younger adults; and other criteria such as certain types of sales promotion appeal mostly to younger shoppers. Older people may also use these criteria or are affected by them differently based on their age. For example, very old people are more likely to be affected by word-of-mouth communication than younger mature consumers. Finally, the importance of the various criteria and the extent to which they have different impacts on various age groups differ by type of product or service. Generally speaking, older consumers' evaluations of various products are influenced by their needs and past experiences. For example, because older people tend to be averse to risk, they value product or store attributes that help them reduce risk such as unconditional guarantees and liberal return policies. Similarly, their declining ability to see, locate, and evaluate merchandise is likely to make them more dependent on salespeople and on informal sources of information. Again, these findings and interpretations point to the need that generalizations should be product- or service-specific. One should avoid generalizing findings in one industry across other industries; also, findings that apply to one product may not apply to other products. Rather, product or service evaluation patterns of older adults should be studied on a product-by-product basis.

In sum, it appears that with age it becomes increasingly difficult for the older person to possess information, and simultaneously there is an increasing need to obtain additional information. How do older persons cope with these conflicting tendencies? Do they use any strategies to compensate for them, or do they become increasingly inefficient in making purchasing decisions? What are some of the important criteria older people consider, and how do these vary by selected sociodemographic and lifestyle characteristics?

Our national survey attempted to provide answers to these questions by assessing older adults' evaluation of products and services in the case of a new product situation. They were asked to respond to four statements regarding purchase of new products (Table 7.1). In buying new products older adults try to evaluate information and avoid risk. Seventy-seven percent agreed with the statement, "I try to learn as much as I can about a new product/service before buying or using it." Only one-third of them admitted that they do not pay attention to product warranties/guarantees, with the majority of them apparently paying close attention to these factors. Despite elaborate information seeking and processing prior to purchase, the largest majority of those 55 years of age and older admitted their inability to evaluate large amounts of information on new products, and about one-third of them admitted they often do not know what to look for in choosing among different brands.

BRAND LOYALTY

One way a person can avoid information processing or product evaluation is to engage in repetitive behavior, that is, to remain "loyal" to the same brand. The prevailing view that older people are brand loyal seems to provide support for this line of reasoning (Hoy and Fisk 1985). Other reasons justifying loyalty to brands among older adults include the belief that older people are set in their ways or that they lack a sense of adventure, and that loyalty to brands helps them reduce risk in purchasing new and relatively unknown products (Hoy and Fisk 1985).

While these arguments have some merit and are intuitively appealing, they lack empirical support. Much of the data point to the opposite conclusion—that is, older people are less likely to be brand loyal. For example, consider the results of the following studies:

- Twenty percent of those age 50 and over tried a new brand of soft drink (Goldring & Co. 1987).

- Brand name was the least important criterion in choosing food products (Schutz, Baird, and Hawkes 1979).

- Analysis of large sets of national data found only a small segment (8.4%) to be brand loyal (Towle and Martin 1976).

While these studies point to the older person's propensity to switch brands, other studies compare brand loyalty between younger and older adults. Their findings support the view that older people are more loyal than their younger counterparts. For example, Zarrel V. Lambert and coauthors (1980) found even low-income elderly not to be prone to choose generic substitutions for brand-name drug products. Also, *The Wall Street Journal's* "American Way of Buying" survey found that people 60 and over are more loyal to brands of cars than their younger counterparts (Ingrassia and Patterson 1989). Finally, we find studies showing that older consumers do not differ markedly from their younger counterparts in their propensity to remain loyal to brands. For example, the Yankelovich Monitor, a market tracing service, found no age differences in answers to the statement "I like to switch brands" (Exter 1986). Similarly, Mark D. Uncles and Andrew S. C. Ehrenberg (1990) found that brand loyalty among older people is not much different than brand loyalty among younger adults.

These findings, indeed, are far from adequate in helping us draw a conclusion. However, when they are evaluated in the context of more recent research, we can suggest three tentative explanations or generalizations. First, brand loyalty may be product or service specific. It might exist for certain types of products or services and not for others, and summarizing results from different studies addressing various types of consumer decisions tends to produce inconclusive evidence. Second, brand loyalty might exist for a limited set of acceptable brands, "allowing" respondents to express both loyalty and switching behavior. Finally, brand loyalty may be a matter of lifestyle and needs. For example, Uncles and Ehrenberg (1990) showed that older adults may be more brand loyal because of their smaller household size and lower frequency of purchase, and differences in brand loyalty disappear when one accounts for such factors.

Our study sought to address the last two issues: Do older people show brand loyalty for a limited number of brands, and how does brand loyalty vary by select characteristics? Our respondents were asked to provide "agree-disagree" answers to three statements (see Table 7.1). Brand loyalty is evident in the responses older adults gave to these three statements. First, more than two-thirds of them agreed that they try to stick to well-known brands. A slightly greater percentage indicated preference for certain brands of most products they buy. Finally, the smallest percentage of the older respondents admitted trying new products every time they are in the store, suggesting loyalty to familiar products or brands.

RESPONSES AMONG YOUNGER AND OLDER ADULTS

In order to gain insight into the behavior of older people (55 and older), responses to statements designed to assess the three types of orientations

Table 7.2
Orientations Toward Products among Younger (under 55) and Older (55+)
Adults (percentage "strongly/somewhat agree")

	Younger	Older
Dissatisfaction with Products and Services		
I sometimes wish I could get my money back for some things I bought	81.2	77.0
Some things I buy do not work as well as they are supposed to	78.4	82.1
I make it a point to let others know of products and services I am not happy with	76.7	73.8
I often find the letters on packages and labels too small to read	31.7	59.6
I often find packages and containers very difficult to open	42.3	69.2
Purchase of New Products		
I try to learn as much as I can about a new product/ service before buying or using it	69.2	77.0
I pay little attention to product warranties and guarantees	25.8	33.5
I often become confused if I have to consider a lot of information about a product I am thinking of buying	30.0	42.8
I often do not know what to look for in choosing among different brands	24.4	34.3
Brand Loyalty		
I try to stick to well-known brands	57.2	66.9
I prefer a certain brand of most products I buy	74.7	70.1
I like to try something new every time I am in the store	18.2	13.5

toward products were compared to those given by the younger age groups. Table 7.2 shows the results of this analysis.

Older and younger adults do not differ greatly in their level of dissatisfaction or satisfaction with products and services, with the exception of their perceptions of size and letters on packages and the ease of opening packages and containers. While younger adults are more likely to regret making certain buying decisions than their older counterparts, they are less likely to report poor product performance (78.4% vs. 82.1%). However, when it comes to their ability to read information on packages and labels, nearly twice as many older adults as younger adults express such a difficulty. A similar significant difference emerged with respect to their ability to open packages and containers, with 69 percent of older adults (versus 42% of younger respondents) expressing concern.

In purchasing new products, responses provided by the two age groups differed markedly, suggesting that older adults may engage in different purchasing processes than their younger counterparts. Older adults tend to be more cautious when buying new products. They are more willing to learn as much as they can about a new product or service before buying or using it, in comparison to their younger counterparts. A larger percentage of older adults, however, admitted that they pay little attention to product guarantees and warranties. As expected, older adults were more likely to admit difficulty in handling a lot of product information, as well as difficulty in knowing what to look for when choosing among different brands.

While older adults tend to stick to well-known brands more than younger adults, they are not as likely as their younger counterparts to prefer a certain brand of most products they buy. Although the percentage of older adults that indicated preference for a certain brand of most products was substantial, it was slightly lower than that for younger adults. Finally, a slightly larger percentage of younger adults than older adults indicated preference for experimentation and variety/novelty-seeking behavior.

To summarize the major findings regarding differences in orientations toward products between younger and older adults, we find that older Americans are relatively more dissatisfied than younger adults with the size of letters on packages and labels and with the ease of opening packages and containers. Also, older adults have a greater difficulty in using product information, despite their willingness and efforts to obtain such information. Finally, older Americans appear to be mostly loyal to a class or set of well-known (national) brands of a product rather than to a specific brand, and they may switch to these brands when they are given the incentive to do so.

SOCIODEMOGRAPHIC DIFFERENCES

In order to address some of the issues raised, responses to various statements related to product orientations were also analyzed only for older adults by age groups (55–64, 65–74, 75+). It was expected that because of the heterogeneity of the mature market, responses might differ due to sociodemographic characteristics.

Several age-related responses emerged from this analysis. Based on these results one can conclude that, with respect to the degree of satisfaction with products and services, with age, there is a slight increase in tendency to regret purchases made. However, there is a decline in the propensity to report poorer product performance than expected, as well as in spreading unfavorable word-of-mouth communication as a result of product dissatisfaction. Finally, ability to read the letters on packages and labels and to open packages and containers declines with age.

The older person's dissatisfaction with products and services cannot be explained merely on the basis of his or her age. Instead, factors that are associated with age such as income and education are likely to affect the way the older person responds to products. For example, regardless of age, middle-income older respondents showed high levels of regret in having bought certain products. In fact, dissatisfaction was highest among middle-income adults age 65 or older; it was lowest among those in the 55-to-64 age bracket in the same income category. However, among upper-income respondents, dissatisfaction declined after age 65. Similarly, expressed difficulty with reading print on packages and with opening packages or containers was related to the older person's income. A significant portion (68.3%) of those in the lower-income bracket of those 65 and over expressed inability to read size of print, in comparison to those in the same age group in middle- and upper-income brackets (51.7% and 55.2%, respectively). Further, difficulty in opening packages and containers was higher among those in the oldest age group who were in the lower-income bracket (75.5%), in comparison with their middle- and upper-income counterparts in the same age group (67.0% and 64.9%, respectively).

There appears to be a curvilinear relationship between age and information utilization in late life. New product information search may be inhibited due to factors such as time pressure prior to retirement years and again very late in life, perhaps due to physical limitations. Attention to product guarantees and warranties declines with age in late life, and so does ability to choose among different brands. Also, with age, there was a reported difficulty in handling large amounts of product information.

However, it is not clear whether these age differences reflect the older person's declining ability to process information due to cognitive deficits or whether these are manifestations of factors associated with age. For example, desire for product information increases with age among respondents in the lower- and upper-income brackets, while propensity to use product information declines with age among those in upper-income brackets (there were no changes with age among older adults in other income brackets). These data suggest that there may be other factors associated with age and income that affect consumer behavior, such as opportunities for consumption and differences in buying experiences as a result of different socioeconomic characteristics.

Finally, with respect to brand loyalty, while the inclination to prefer well-known brands increases slightly with age, the tendency to buy certain brands for most products purchased declines. Collectively, these responses suggest frequent loyalty or brand switching only to well-known brands as one ages.

However, while a larger percentage of upper-income older adults (65+) (77.4%) expressed preference for well-known brands, a relatively smaller percentage of them expressed preference for buying the same brand (63.3%). These numbers compare with 68.7 percent and 72.5 percent for middle-income older adults and with 70.1 percent and 68.0 percent for the lower-income groups, respectively. Thus, brand switching to well-known brands and lower loyalty appear to be characteristic mostly of upper-income older Americans.

Given the possible confounding factors such as income, the effects of age were also analyzed by taking into consideration the many factors that are associated with age. Again, the intent of this analysis was to remove any contaminating influences of other age-related variables on the findings of the effects of age per se. The results of this additional analysis suggest minimal differences due to age, when a host of other variables were assessed for their effects simultaneously. Only one's ability to open packages and containers and, to a lesser extent, one's ability to read the size of letters on labels and packages declines with age. These declines might in fact reflect a physiological decline in vision and manual dexterity. With respect to purchasing new products, there appears to be a decline in knowledge to use criteria crucial in product selection. Finally, there are virtually no differences in brand loyalty with age in late life. Collectively, these findings suggest that many age differences in response to products in late life may be results of many factors associated with age, rather than the result of age per se.

Our study also explored the possibility that responses to products and services may vary by gender. Therefore, responses given by older males were compared to those given by older females. Female older adults were found to be somewhat more likely than their male counterparts to regret having made certain purchases and to express dissatisfaction with the performance of some products. Similarly, a much larger percentage (75.2%) of female mature consumers indicated that they often find packages and containers very difficult to open, in comparison to their male counterparts (60.9%). These differences in responses may not be due to gender per se—that is, males being physically stronger than females—but rather the result of lifestyle and buying roles that prevail in society. For example, the fact that females find packages and containers more difficult to open may be because more older women in general are likely to handle such products due to differences in family role structure. Finally, with respect to purchasing new products, females were more likely to indicate difficulty in handling large amounts of information (50.4%), in comparison with their male counterparts (32.7%). Finally, females expressed a slightly

greater inclination to prefer a certain brand of most products they buy than their male counterparts (73.3% versus 67.1%).

While there was no reason to expect geographic differences in responses, such an analysis was performed simply for exploratory purposes in order to address some of the issues raised. Some geographic differences did emerge. In examining responses to statements related to dissatisfaction or satisfaction with products and services, a larger percentage of westerners (83.1%) than southerners (75.7%) and northerners (74.8%) showed regret making some purchases. A higher percentage of easterners (83.6%) than older adults living in northern states (69.9%) and western states (72.5%) said they are likely to complain to others when they experience unsatisfactory purchases. Also, easterners are somewhat more likely to find the letters on packages and labels too small to read than older adults living in northern states (64.1% versus 55.0%). When it comes to purchasing new products, a relatively large percentage of those living in the south (39.1%) reported they were likely not to pay attention to product warranties or guarantees, while westerners were most likely to report that they pay attention to these factors (26.1%). The remaining geographic differences were negligible, but the reader should be reminded that the geographic regions formed are very broad groupings.

Another consideration in our research was the examination of differences in responses to products by level of income. We arbitrarily broke down our respondents' income levels into three categories: under $30,000 (low), $30,000–$49,999 (middle), and $50,000 or more (high). Satisfaction with products and services appears to increase somewhat with level of income. For example, there was a tendency to report less regret of purchases among higher-income older adults, although complaining to others did not appear to be affected by income. Upper-income mature consumers reported greater difficulty in reading information on packages and labels, suggesting that such responses may not be merely due to vision loss but due to other factors associated with income such as education. The same trend appeared to occur with respect to the mature person's ability to open packages and containers. Again, factors such as education may be directly responsible for these differences, since lower educated respondents may not make use of product information or use efficient ways to open packages, in comparison with their upscale counterparts. Ability to use and handle product information increases with income, and so does the older person's tendency to report inability to choose among different brands of products. There were minimal variations in brand loyalty due to income of older adults.

ORIENTATIONS BY NEED-BASED GROUPS

It was expected that needs characterizing the consumption process would underlie many of the responses given to products and services.

Need-based clusters (see Appendix F), therefore, were examined for their responses to the three types of orientations toward products and services. While there were relatively few differences in responses among the four need-based clusters, some are worth mentioning. First, the dependent frail group was most likely to report difficulty in reading information on packages and labels, with 61.6 percent of them indicating this problem, compared with 52.8 percent of struggling full-nesters. Similarly, the dependent frail were more likely to find packages and containers difficult to open (68.3%) in comparison to struggling full-nesters (58.5%).

Dependent frail were also more likely than young insecureds to ignore product warranties and guarantees (37.3% versus 30.3%). Finally, self-sufficients composed the group most likely to exhibit preference for well-known brands (71.0%) in comparison to young insecureds who were least likely to report such preferences (58.4%). Young insecureds were also less likely to show preferences for products they buy (64.9%) in comparison with nearly 74 percent of struggling full-nesters.

In sum, responses to products and services do not show much variability among need-based clusters, whether these responses are evaluated as dissatisfaction or satisfaction with products or services, purchase of new products, or brand orientations.

PRODUCT ORIENTATIONS BY GERONTOGRAPHIC SEGMENTS

While need-based groups do not respond differently to products, groups defined in terms of gerontographic characteristics appear to show a much greater variability in responses. Table 7.3 presents responses to the same product-related orientations by gerontographic cluster.

With respect to dissatisfaction with products and services, healthy hermits show a consistently higher satisfaction level than other groups. Specifically, individuals in this group are less likely to regret making a purchase than healthy indulgers, and they are not as likely as frail recluses to report product performance below their expectations. Although there are no significant differences between their propensity to complain to others and that of respondents in other gerontographic groups, a smaller percentage of healthy hermits than other groups, such as ailing outgoers and frail recluses, express difficulty in reading packages and labels. They are also less likely than frail recluses to find packages and containers difficult to open.

Gerontographic segments also show several variations in responses to buying new products. For example, while ailing outgoers are most likely to try to learn a lot about new products before buying them, a relatively smaller percentage of frail recluses are likely to do the same. Similarly, while 57 percent of ailing outgoers pay little attention to product warranties and guarantees, 49 percent of healthy hermits are likely to report the

Table 7.3
Orientations Toward Products by Gerontographic Clusters (percentage "strongly/somewhat agree")

	Healthy Hermits	Ailing Outgoers	Frail Recluses	Healthy Indulgers
Dissatisfaction with Products and Services				
I sometimes wish I could get my money back for some things I bought	66.03	82.64	77.70	83.46
Some things I buy do not work as well as they are supposed to	76.44	82.64	83.11	80.31
I make it a point to let others know of products and services I am not happy with	73.15	79.42	74.32	73.23
I often find the letters on packages and labels too small to read	50.68	65.59	62.84	59.84
I often find packages and containers difficult to open	60.55	67.20	72.97	62.99
Purchase of New Products				
I try to learn as much as I can about a new product/service before buying or using it	76.21	81.03	68.92	77.17
I pay little attention to product warranties and guarantees	49.04	57.23	52.03	51.18
I often become confused if I have to consider a lot of information about a product I am thinking of buying	40.55	30.87	23.65	37.01
I often do not know what to look for in choosing among different brands	47.95	32.80	40.54	46.46
Brand Loyalty				
I try to stick to well-known brands	65.75	68.49	67.57	65.35
I prefer a certain brand of most products I buy	66.30	70.74	65.54	73.23
I like to try something new every time I am in the store	11.78	16.40	8.78	14.96

same orientation. On the other hand, healthy hermits are nearly twice as likely as frail recluses to indicate difficulty in processing large amounts of information about products. A larger percentage of healthy hermits also report inability in using proper criteria in selecting among brands, in comparison to ailing outgoers.

Some variability in responses is also evident with respect to brand loyalty, with the healthy indulgers being the group most likely to show preference for certain brands of most products they buy, and frail recluses the group least likely to do so. Frail recluses show lower incidence of buying new products and experimentation than other gerontographic groups, especially ailing outgoers.

SUMMARY AND IMPLICATIONS

To summarize, older consumers tend to be dissatisfied with products and services, but their discontent is generally shared also by younger adults. Age-related differences found may not be due to age per se but due to other factors associated with age. In fact, age itself appears to explain very little in responses to products and services among older adults. Some variations in responses exist across other characteristics such as sex, income, and geographic location. The causes for these differences are not clear.

One major source of dissatisfaction among adult shoppers is their inability to read information on packages and labels. Given that recent legislation calls for more information on products, it is highly unlikely that the size of letters on labels and packages will increase, contributing to the existing problem. Manufacturers must seek alternative ways to provide information to the older person. For example, product-use directions could be printed in larger print and placed inside the package. Alternatively, manufacturers and service providers could form alliances to meet the consumption needs of older consumers. For example, food manufacturers and household appliance makers could work together to develop systems, such as automatic programming of ovens to cook certain foods based on information electronically retrieved from food packages. Our national study further revealed that dissatisfaction with information on packages and labels is not due to age per se but relates to various characteristics of the older person. For example, those who expressed greatest concern with this problem tended to be the oldest, to live in eastern states, and to be at the extreme of income brackets (high and low income). They are most likely to belong to the dependent frail need-based cluster and to be either ailing outgoers or frail recluses.

Another major source of older consumer dissatisfaction is the difficulty they experience with opening packages and containers. This problem can be alleviated by developing packaging that is easier to open. However, it should be noted that dissatisfaction in this area is highest among older consumers who are very old, who are female, who are most likely to belong to dependent frail and struggling full-nesters need-based groups, and who have the gerontographic profile of frail recluses.

Although older adults are likely to seek information in order to make the best choice, they often have difficulty in choosing among products.

Although older adults make a greater effort than their younger counterparts to gather and use more product information, they are handicapped in the way they use it. They are likely to make mistakes, regret making purchases and feel frustrated because the product/service does not live up to their expectations. These findings suggest the need for improving the presentation format of information on packages and labels. One way to assist older shoppers is to study how their information processing abilities change with age and to examine alternative formats of information that would make their shopping task more effective and less cumbersome. This information could then be incorporated into packaging. However, it should be noted that the older person's ability to use information and make wise decisions is also a matter of certain characteristics. By understanding the characteristics of older adults most likely to be in need of information, marketers can make a greater effort to satisfy such information needs. For example, the research presented here suggests that female older adults have greater difficulty than do their male counterparts in handling large amounts of information when making purchasing decisions. The same appears to be the case for the lower-income older consumers. Frail recluses are the gerontographic group most likely to report difficulty in processing large amounts of information, and healthy hermits are most likely to report an inability in using proper criteria in selecting among brands.

With respect to the criteria used by older consumers, the research presented in this chapter suggests that older people do not necessarily use any strategies to compensate for their declining abilities to gather and process information. For example, attention to product guarantees and warranties declines with age, and older consumers report difficulty in choosing among brands. It is not clear that older adults even use simple strategies such as purchasing only well-known brands. This research further suggests that one's perceived importance of criteria such as guarantees and warranties is not only a matter of age but is also influenced by a large number of factors. For example, the older subgroups most likely to consider these criteria tend to live in western states, are dependent frail, and are healthy hermits.

Some variability in responses was found among people from various income levels, with upper-income older adults being more likely to purchase new products more efficiently than lower-income older adults. Age appeared to make little difference in the way older adults respond to new products as well as in brand loyalty tendencies. With respect to the issue of brand loyalty, the research presented suggests that older people are likely to switch to a limited number of well-known brands. Furthermore, brand loyalty is likely to vary little across sociodemographic and need-based clusters, but gerontographic groups do differ in this regard.

Finally, with respect to the issue of market segmentation, while psychographic groups based on consumption-related needs do not show significant differences in responses, gerontographic segments show a greater efficacy in predicting older adults' orientations toward products. These findings suggest the desirability of using gerontographics to segment the mature market.

8

Identifying and Targeting Potential Users of New Products

The area of new product adoption has been an important concern to marketers for two main reasons. First, new products must be continuously developed and successfully introduced to the market if the firm is to achieve long-term survival and profitability. Second, products introduced to the marketplace experience high failure rates, or the number of adopters is not large enough to help the firm recover its production and marketing costs. The area is of additional importance in marketing to the older population because, in comparison to younger consumers, older consumers are much more heterogeneous. Therefore, it is more difficult to estimate demand potential and appeal to the older consumer market. Furthermore, older consumers are traditionally considered to be averse to new products.

The purpose of this chapter is to provide answers to a number of questions related to new product adoption. First, the issue of older consumer acceptance of new products is raised and addressed using findings from previous studies. Next, data from our national study are used to address older consumers' orientations toward new technologies and to supplement/expand existing knowledge. Third, a profile of older adults who are potential users of new technological innovations is developed to aid marketers in identifying and targeting potential adopters.

ACCEPTANCE OF NEW PRODUCTS

While conventional wisdom suggests that older people are not likely to buy new products and services, recent studies show that older persons may accept innovations, but there are differences in their propensity to embrace new products and services. These differences can be attributed to a number of factors. Some of these factors relate to characteristics of older adults, while others have to do with the innovations or environmental circumstances. First, differences in consumers' propensity to buy new products may be due to factors associated with age. One such factor is education. Those most likely to respond to new technologies are expected to be those who understand them—that is, the most educated. Older people on the whole do not have as much education as younger people, and as a result they do not respond as favorably to new products and ideas. This argument is supported by data presented by Richard Prisuta and Robert Kriner (1985). Another reason for the lower inclination to accept many new technologies in late life may be related to the gradual decline of the central nervous system, which begins at about age 45. The increasing deficiency in the neurological system is likely to be associated with the aging person's orientation toward new technologies, as they are likely to experience difficulty in information gathering and processing regarding unfamiliar stimuli (Moschis 1992b).

Another set of factors likely to affect the older individual's propensity to accept new products and ideas relate to the innovation itself. For example, familiarity with existing technologies probably increases the likelihood of adoption of a new technological innovation (Moschis 1992b).

One of the interesting findings of Prisuta and Kriner's (1985) study was that age is not a significant factor in explaining attitudes. The reason older people had a negative attitude toward new technologies is because of their lower levels of education and income, not age per se. A study by Paul A. Kerschner and Kathleen A. Chelsving (1981) found older adults to be less likely than their younger counterparts to use innovations such as automatic bank-teller machines (ATMs), calculators, video recorders, video games, and cable television. In the same study, age was found to be negatively associated with attitudes toward technology.

Another study by Mary C. Gilly and Valarie A. Zeithaml (1985) investigated adoption of several key consumer-related technologies in elderly (65+) and nonelderly samples. The elderly were found to be less likely to adopt most innovations (scanner-equipped grocery stores, ATMs, and custom telephone calling services) but they were more likely to adopt electronic funds transfer. In a study of consumer acceptance of Lifeline telephone emergency response service, inventor Andrew S. Dibner and his coworkers found 65 percent of the frail elderly accepted the system when offered. Once on the system, 88 percent held positive attitudes toward it, and 29 percent elected to pay to continue it at the end of demonstration of the project. Continuers had more serious medical conditions and had used the system at twice the rate of noncontinuers to obtain help in emergencies (Dibner, Lowy, and Morris 1982). A national study conducted by the Center for Mature Consumer Studies (CMCS) for Whirlpool Corporation (Moschis et al. 1991) also found high acceptance of certain technological innovations among adults age 55 and older. For example, nearly nine in ten respondents age 55 and older indicated ownership or use of microwave ovens. Similarly, Donnelley Marketing found people age 50 and older to be as favorably disposed toward new technology as those age 25 to 49 (Balkite 1988).

Another study by Daniel Yankelovich for the Markle Foundation (1988) provided a different perspective for the differences found between younger and older adults in their propensity to embrace new consumer technologies—VCRs, ATM banking, microwave ovens, and the like. According to this study, to middle-aged Americans (age 45 to 59), these technologies provide the immediate benefits of saving time or allowing them to shift time (bank at midnight, tape a TV show for viewing later). For older adults, on the other hand, who have plenty of free time and seek "time fillers" (things to do to keep them busy), such technologies are not viewed favorably. These innovations are geared toward providing convenience, and older Americans concerned with filling their time reject convenience as an obstacle to an active lifestyle.

The diffusion literature reviewed by Hubert Gatignon and Thomas S. Robertson (1985) also suggested that an innovation is more likely to be adopted when consumers can see the benefits associated with it, either because it helps one do something better than the existing products or services (relative advantage) or because it fits into the consumer's established pattern of consumption (compatibility). This might help explain the different levels of adoption of various types of technological innovations by older adults. That is, those innovations that provide direct benefits to the older consumer because of their compatibility with existing needs (electronic funds transfer [EFT], electronic hearing aids) are more readily accepted, while those that do not offer direct benefits (video games, personal computers) are losers in gaining popularity among the older population (Moschis 1992b). Thus, for example, a person who does not have a hearing problem is not likely to use a new hearing device no matter how innovation-prone that person might be. Similarly, a person who receives few phone calls or does not spend time outside his or her home is unlikely to have an interest in custom calling telephone services, such as "call waiting."

The CMCS study for Whirlpool Corporation (Moschis et al. 1991) provided additional insight into the older person's orientations toward new products and their adoption of them. The study asked respondents, including 258 older adults age 55 to 64 and 390 age 65 or older to indicate whether they presently have/use, have tried, have considered using, have heard of, or have never heard of ten products and services. Based on the study's results, high-tech products and services that offer convenience or save time led mature consumers' ownership and use list. More than nine in ten (92.9%) of the older respondents age 55 to 64 indicated ownership or use of a microwave oven, in comparison to those in the under 55 age group (92.7%); for the oldest group (65+) the percentage of those who have access to a microwave oven was lower (86.0%). Videocassette recorders were also found to be widely accepted by the older population, with four in five (81.1%) of the 55-to-64 age group and a little over half (52.5%) of those age 65 and older reporting ownership or use. Use of EFT increases with age, with nearly two-thirds of the oldest group reporting adoption. Cordless phones were also reported to be present in many older households; nearly half (45.1%) of the 55-to-64 age group and one-third of the older group reported ownership or use. Ownership or use of telephone answering machines drops after age 65, while adults under age 55 are twice as likely as those in the older group to report use of ATMs. Even new products and services that had not been widely adopted by the mature consumer market had a high level of awareness among this sample. Except for Retin-A and the AT&T Universal Credit Card, at least nine in ten adults age 55 and older reported being aware of the availability of new products and services. (Given that at the time of the survey AT&T Universal had issued only 5 million credit cards, it is possible that a relatively large percentage of older adults may have mistaken the card for AT&T's regular telephone credit card for use of long distance services.) For products and services that show sizeable use by mature consumers, many respondents reported trying them, but for various reasons discontinued use. Nearly one-quarter of the 55-and-over sample had tried premium cable channels and cordless phones but discontinued using them. About one in ten mature adults had experimented with ATMs and found them lacking in some way.

The older person's orientation toward technological innovations might reflect different stages in the disengagement process and, therefore, orientations toward the services provided through the new technologies rather than toward the technologies themselves. For example, because of isolation and withdrawal from a more active role in society (such as travel and social events), a person's assumption of a more confined role might reduce the number of needs that can be satisfied through technological innovations. The low use of custom-calling telephone services found by Gilly and Zeithaml (1985) may indeed reflect limited need for these services, as indicated by the open-ended comments of their respondents. It is also possible that a younger person in the household (for example, an adult child) owns or uses the new products. This could explain the sharp drop in ownership or use after age 65, since many older households are likely to be "empty-nested."

Finally, age-related differences (or no differences) in responses to technological innovations may be due to the way information is obtained from consumers. Acceptance of technological innovations has been assessed at different levels of consumer response, including attitudes and actual use.

When attitudes toward new technologies are assessed, older and younger people tend to show favorable orientation or few differences in responses. For example, the Prisuta and Kriner (1985) study found few age differences. Similarly, the study by Donnelley Marketing (Balkite 1988) found older adults to be favorably predisposed toward new technologies. On the other hand, when actual behavior is taken into account, there are likely to be several age-related differences. Thus, older adults may give "socially desirable" responses when they are asked to indicate their opinions about new technologies, overstating their feelings and opinions about such products.

To summarize the results of previous studies, older adults' relatively low interest in new products may be due to their withdrawal from active lifestyles. However, the reasons older people do not readily accept most new products or services are not very clear. There is some evidence suggesting that older consumers are likely to adopt new products and services when they see benefits in using them.

ORIENTATIONS TOWARD TECHNOLOGIES

Our national study sought to provide additional evidence on this topic. Specifically, it examined three types of orientations toward technologies: attitudes toward high-tech products, use/ownership of recent technological innovations, and purchase likelihood of emerging or new products and services, many of which are high-tech based.

Attitudes Toward Technologies

Attitudes toward technologies were assessed by asking the respondents in the survey to agree or disagree with three statements. One statement dealt with perceptions of technology's effects on life, another dealt with perceived difficulty in dealing with electronic products, and the last dealt with the effects of electronic products on the life of older adults. Older people were divided with respect to their attitudes toward technologies. While a large percentage of older adults (39.2%) were of the opinion that technology has not made life easier, an equally large percentage of the respondents age 55 and older (43.9%) did not feel that using electronic products is too confusing to bother with. Finally, the overwhelming majority (71.8%) agreed that older people should learn to use electronic gadgets and services that can make their lives easier.

Although older adults have rather positive attitudes toward technologies, their attitudes differ markedly from those of adults under age 55, with younger adults having even more positive attitudes than older adults toward high-tech products. However, younger people are less likely to have the opinion that high-tech products be used by older adults, compared to the opinions of their older counterparts.

With respect to possible effects of other characteristics of older adults, our study revealed that attitudes toward technologies tend to become less favorable with age. Males had more positive attitudes toward technologies than their female counterparts. Older adults living in northern and western states were more likely than their easterner counterparts to show positive attitudes toward high-tech products. Income made no difference in older adults' attitudes toward technologies.

Finally, attitudes toward technologies were examined among need-based clusters and gerontographic groups. Significant differences in responses emerged only with respect to the first statement. Struggling full-nesters had the least negative opinions on the effects of technological improvements on life, while the young insecureds gave the most negative opinions. However, this was not the case when responses by gerontographic groups were considered. Significant variations on each of the three statements emerged. Specifically, healthy hermits had the most negative attitudes toward the effects of technology on life, while frail recluses had the least negative attitudes (41.6% versus 25.0%, respectively). On the other hand, healthy hermits were the group least likely to admit that electronic products are too confusing to bother with (21.1%), in comparison to the remaining three groups. Even attitudes toward use of technologies by older people varied by gerontographic group, with a larger percentage of healthy indulgers (77.9%) and ailing outgoers (76.8%) than frail recluses (65.5%) and healthy hermits (67.7%) responding favorably.

Collectively, these findings point to rather weak and confounding effects of demographics and psychographics (defined in terms of needs) and suggest the usefulness of gerontographic characteristics in predicting favorable responses toward technologies.

Ownership and Use of Recent Technologies

Responses were also obtained on five relatively recent innovations: ATMs, EFT, custom telephone-calling services (CTCS), cable TV, and cordless phones. The first four were similar to those used by Gilly and Zeithaml (1985); they were used for 'validation" of this sample and the study results with those of previous studies.

Generally, these findings (see Table 8.1) are consistent with those of previous research. (For comparison, see Gilly and Zeithaml 1985.) Furthermore, we noted an increase in use of ATMs only among the elderly, and in CTCS only among the nonelderly; there was also an increase in EFT in both groups over the previous five years. In addition, there were wide geographic variations in use/ownership of recently introduced technologies among older adults. More than one-third (35.4%) of our sample

Table 8.1
Interest in Recently Introduced Technological Innovations among Younger
(under 55) and Older (55+) Adults (percentage "very/somewhat interested")

	Younger	Older
Automated Bank Teller Machines--(ATMs) (N = 921)	33.03	16.79
Electronic Fund Transfer (Automatic deposit of your check--EFT) (N = 930)	29.31	22.94
Custom Telephone Calling Services - (like "call waiting" and "call forwarding") (N = 1,180)	33.42	15.08
Cable TV (N = 593)	56.39	35.93
Cordless phone (N = 1,007)	50.12	30.09

living in western states reported use of ATMs in comparison with a little over 20 percent among those in northern states. A similar conclusion can be reached with respect to the use of EFT services, although easterners showed a relatively low use of this service as well. The penetration of CTCS was the highest among older adults living in western states (16.2%) in comparison to those living in eastern states (9.8%). Westerners, however, reported the lowest ownership/use of cable TV and cordless phones of any of the remaining geographic groups.

Adoption of New/Emerging Products and Services

Older respondents in our sample expressed preferences for the thirteen emerging or new products/services, including several technological innovations, in the form of (a) likelihood of purchase and (b) the highest price they would pay. Table 8.2 shows percentage distributions of responses to various levels of purchase likelihood.

The medical ID card appears to be the most preferred concept, followed by the two types of alarm systems. Half of older Americans age 55 and older indicated they would definitely or probably use a medical ID card that can be electronically read by medical staff in case of emergency to show them useful medical information (like conditions, allergies, doctors, and medications). One-third of older adults indicated high likelihood of using an alarm system that would monitor their home, check undesirable conditions, and notify the appropriate person or emergency unit. Nearly

Table 8.2
Adoption Likelihood of New Products and Services

	Definitely/ Probably Would not Buy %	Might Buy %	Definitely/ Probably Would Buy %
An electronic calendar in your watch or telephone that would remind you to do certain things	65.5	20.8	13.7
A telephone number that would connect you with a small number of people wishing to have conversation on a variety of topics on given dates and times	85.5	9.1	5.4
Ability to request certain TV programs to be aired at any time you wanted to watch them	53.4	24.7	21.7
Ability to pay all utility bills in one bill, with the total amount automatically subtracted from your bank account or charged to your bank card	67.5	13.9	18.6
A club providing services such as volunteer programs, courses, jobs for retirees and social activities such as "fashion shows for all ages"	57.8	24.3	17.8
An alarm system that would monitor your personal health, diagnose undesirable conditions and alert you or automatically notify an emergency unit	40.8	30.1	29.1
An alarm system that would monitor your personal home, check undesirable conditions and notify the appropriate person or emergency unit	37.7	27.7	34.4
Product demonstrations on TV that can be ordered via phone (or home computer) and delivered to your home	82.4	12.2	5.3
Community vans that will give you a ride to and from shopping centers, doctors, church, etc.	56.6	26.1	17.3
Directories of individuals willing to trade services	64.2	22.8	12.7
Special assistance phone numbers, with the operator helping in locating the nearest certified person available to provide a service (like repairs)	53.4	28.6	18.1
A medical ID card that can be electronically read by medical staff in case of emergency to show them useful information (like conditions, allergies, doctors, and medications)	21.1	28.1	50.8
Directories of numbers which you can call to get prerecorded information on various topics, such as special events, store sales, vacation packages, and financial and medical news	60.3	21.8	17.9

one in ten expressed interest in using an alarm system that would monitor their personal health, diagnose undesirable conditions and alert them or automatically notify an emergency unit. About one in five would use a service that would allow them to request certain TV programs to be aired at any time they wanted to watch them. Nearly one in five older Americans indicated inclination to use five other services. In order to determine penetration rates, an index of relative likelihood of purchase across the thirteen products/services was computed for each. The computation of penetration rates is based on the assumption that a larger percentage of those indicating high likelihood of purchase will actually purchase the product than among those indicating low purchase likelihood. Specifically, responses (in percentages) were weighted by 0.9, 0.7, 0.5, 0.3, and 0.1, assuming that 90 percent of those who said that they "definitely would buy" will actually buy/use, 70 percent of those who said "probably would" actually will, and so forth for the remaining three categories. The results of these computations along with the highest price older consumers are willing to pay (on the average) are shown in Table 8.3.

PROFILING THE POTENTIAL USER

Table 8.4 shows responses to the new products and services among younger and older (55+) adults. Younger adults are more likely than their older counterparts to report intentions to use an electronic calender, pay-per-view cable services, one bill for all utilities, direct ordering products via TV, special-assistance phone numbers, and audiotext (prerecorded messages). On the other hand, older adults are more likely than their younger counterparts to use a club that provides various services and community vans. The remaining products and services are about equally preferred by both age groups. Thus, although the thirteen products/services were developed to satisfy older consumer needs, the majority were preferred by younger adults. It is possible that younger adults may want to purchase some of these products for their older relatives, but we have no way of determining the extent to which responses by younger adults reflect their own needs for such products vis-à-vis perceived needs of others.

If many of these new/emerging innovations are of greater appeal to certain segments of older consumers, can those who are most likely to adopt them be identified and profiled for marketing purposes? In our research we used a number of characteristics to profile potential users of innovations. These characteristics are: use of other recently introduced innovations, sociodemographic characteristics, need-based lifestyles, and gerontographics.

Use of Recent Innovations

Responses to each of the five innovations (see Table 8.1) were tabulated by usage probability of the thirteen emerging innovations. By examining percentage differences among users and nonusers, a profile of the potential user can be developed with respect to probable use of each of the thirteen new products and services.

Table 8.3
Penetration Rates and Highest Price Willing to Pay for New Products/Services

	Penetration Rate %	Average Highest Price $
An electronic calendar in your watch or telephone that would remind you to do certain things	33.13	33.75
A telephone number that would connect you with a small number of people wishing to have conversation on a variety of topics on given dates and times	23.04	1.94 (per call)
Ability to request certain TV programs to be aired at any time you wanted to watch them	39.16	2.80 (per program)
Ability to pay all utility bills in one bill, with the total amount automatically subtracted from your bank account or charged to your bank card	33.00	10.77 (per month)
A club providing services such as volunteer programs, courses, jobs for retirees and social activities such as "fashion shows for all ages"	34.16	21.03 (per year)
An alarm system that would monitor your personal health, diagnose undesirable conditions and alert you or automatically notify an emergency unit	45.94	746.18
An alarm system that would monitor your personal home, check undesirable conditions and notify the appropriate person or emergency unit	48.68	243.99
Product demonstrations on TV that can be ordered via phone (or home computer) and delivered to your home	23.13	4.50 (per month)
Community vans that will give you a ride to and from shopping centers, doctors, church, etc.	38.14	11.48 (per month)
Directories of individuals willing to trade services	32.57	8.07 (per year)
Special assistance phone numbers, with the operator helping in locating the nearest certified person available to provide a service (like repairs)	39.21	1.36 (per call)
A medical ID card that can be electronically read by medical staff in case of emergency to show them useful information (like conditions, allergies, doctors, and medications)	59.26	13.40 (for a new or updated card)
Directories of numbers which you can call to get prerecorded information on various topics, such as special events, store sales, vacation packages, and financial and medical news	35.80	1.22 (per call)

The *electronic calendar* is most likely to appeal to those mature consumers who own a cordless phone and use cable TV. *Open-talk* services are likely to appeal to those who presently use CTCS and own a cordless phone. *TV programs* at request of viewers are likely to be preferred by users of CTCS and cordless phone owners. Preference for *one bill for all*

Table 8.4
Adoption Likelihood of New/Emerging Products and Services by Younger (under 55) and Older (55+) Adults

	Younger %	Older %
An electronic calendar in your watch or telephone that would remind you to do certain things	22.3	13.6
A telephone number that would connect you with a small number of people wishing to have conversation on a variety of topics on given dates and times	6.4	5.7
Ability to request certain TV programs to be aired at any time you wanted to watch them	43.0	20.1
Ability to pay all utility bills in one bill, with the total amount automatically subtracted from your bank account or charged to your bank card	29.2	19.0
A club providing services such as volunteer programs, courses, jobs for retirees and social activities such as "fashion shows for all ages"	10.8	17.4
An alarm system that would monitor your personal health, diagnose undesirable conditions and alert you or automatically notify an emergency unit	24.2	27.0
An alarm system that would monitor your home, check undesirable conditions and notify the appropriate person or emergency unit	35.2	32.7
Product demonstrations on TV that can be ordered via phone (or home computer) and delivered to your home	10.0	5.5
Community vans that will give you a ride to and from shopping centers, doctors, church, etc.	10.0	16.7
Directories of individuals willing to trade services	22.9	11.9
Special assistance phone numbers, with the operator helping in locating the nearest certified person available to provide a service (like repairs)	22.9	11.9
A medical ID card that can be electronically read by medical staff in case of emergency to show them useful information (like conditions, allergies, doctors, and medications)	45.2	48.2
Directories of numbers which you can call to get prerecorded information on various topics, such as special events, store sales, vacation packages, and financial and medical news	24.9	17.4

utilities is most likely to be shown by present users of ATMs, EFT, and cable TV. A *club* providing services is likely to be of greater appeal to ATM users than to nonusers. A *health-monitoring alarm system* is likely to appeal to CTCS users. Preferences for the remaining seven (of thirteen) emerging innovations cannot be accurately predicted by usage of existing five innovations.

Sociodemographic Characteristics

A number of sociodemographic characteristics can be used to develop a profile of older adults who are most likely to adopt new or emerging technologies. Using the information gathered in our study, interest in the thirteen new or emerging products and services was analyzed by several factors. Among those age 55 or older, the study found a declining interest with age in ordering specific TV programs as well as in joining a club that provides various services. On the other hand, interest in having access to community vans for transportation increases with age. No significant differences emerged across respondents by level of income in nearly all the thirteen products studied, with the exception of community vans where usage likelihood was inversely related to income. Responses to emerging products and services varied significantly by sex for only four of the thirteen new concepts. Specifically, male older adults were more likely than their female counterparts to express likelihood of adopting the electronic calendar as well as the concept of paying for all utility bills in one bill. Women, on the other hand, were more likely to express usage likelihood for the club that provides services as well as for community vans.

Responses to new/emerging products and services were also analyzed by geographic region to determine the extent to which older adults who live in various parts of the country show different orientations toward these products and services. A larger percentage of older adults who live in the west, in comparison to those who live in the north (15.5% versus 11.3%), expressed a high adoption likelihood of the electronic calendar. However, a smaller percentage (17.9%) of older adults who live in the north, in comparison to those who live in the east (24.0%) and west (23.6%), expressed interest in TV programs that can be aired at preferred times. A club providing services is more likely to be preferred by older adults who live in the east than among those who live in the north (20.2% vs. 15.6%). Easterners are also more likely to adopt a health-monitoring system than northerners, with 34.1 percent and 23.5 percent expressing preference, respectively. Furthermore, easterners are more likely than their counterparts in the other three geographic groups to indicate purchase or usage likelihood for the home-monitoring system, with 40.2 percent of them expressing definite or probable adoption likelihood, compared with 29.9 percent of northerners, 31.7 percent of southerners, and 34.6 percent of westerners.

While a relatively small percentage of older adults in general expressed interest in product demonstrations on TV, westerners were more likely than southerners (4.7% versus 1.0%) to express such preferences. Easterners were more likely than westerners to indicate adoption plans for community vans, with 21.3 percent and 13.9 percent, respectively, indicating an intention to use. Easterners are nearly twice as likely as northerners and southerners to show preference for directories of individuals willing to trade services, with 18.9 percent of them (versus 10.5 percent and 9.6 percent, respectively) indicating such preferences. Special-assistance numbers are also of greater value to easterners, with 23.7 percent indicating usage intentions, compared to 13.6 percent of the northerners. Also, a larger percentage of easterners (57.0%) than northerners (48.1%) and southerners (43.7%) expressed intentions to use a medical ID card, and a larger percentage of easterners than southerners (22.8% versus 13.3%) expressed intentions to use the directories with audiotext services.

Lifestyles and Adoption of New Products/Services

Responses to new or emerging products and services differed across the four need-based lifestyles. One in five struggling full-nesters, compared to almost one in ten (11.9%) dependent frail, expressed interest in an electronic calendar that would remind them to do certain things. Twice as many young insecureds as self-sufficients (8.6% versus 4.3%) indicated interest in open talk. A club providing services was preferred by a larger percentage of struggling full-nesters (17.1%) than dependent frail (11.2%). More than one in three (35.1%) young insecureds, in comparison with one in four (26.5%) dependent frail, would use a home alarm system. Struggling full-nesters are more likely than their dependent frail counterparts to use directories of individuals willing to trade services (14.6% and 9.7%, respectively). In sum, differences in five of the thirteen products and services studied were found across need-based lifestyles, suggesting that these groups might be useful in helping marketers develop profiles of potential new product users.

New Product Adoption by Gerontographic Groups

Responses to new or emerging products and services varied significantly across gerontographic groups. Table 8.5 shows that the electronic calendar and open talk are of greater appeal to ailing outgoers than to healthy hermits. The former group is also more likely than the latter to indicate usage likelihood regarding TV viewing of programs at certain times. Ability to pay all utility bills in one bill is of greater interest to healthy in-

Table 8.5
Adoption Likelihood of New Products and Services by Gerontographic Clusters
(percentage "definitely/probably would use")

	Healthy Hermits	Ailing Outgoers	Frail Recluses	Healthy Indulgers
An electronic calendar in your watch or telephone that would remind you to do certain things	11.78	20.90	16.89	14.96
A telephone number that would connect you with a small number of people wishing to have conversation on a variety of topics on given dates and times	2.74	8.68	6.08	6.30
Ability to request certain TV programs to be aired at any time you wanted to watch them	16.16	27.97	19.59	18.90
Ability to pay all utility bills in one bill, with the total amount automatically subtracted from your bank account or charged to your bank card	18.36	22.83	20.95	24.41
A club providing services such as volunteer programs, courses, jobs for retirees and social activities such as "fashion shows for all ages"	10.68	21.22	11.49	16.54
An alarm system that would monitor your personal health, diagnose undesirable conditions and alert you or automatically notify an emergency unit	16.44	40.51	29.05	27.56
An alarm system that would monitor your home, check undesirable conditions and notify the appropriate person or emergency unit	25.48	40.84	26.35	37.80
Product demonstrations on TV that can be ordered via phone (or home computer) and delivered to your home	3.29	7.72	7.43	4.72
Community vans that will give you a ride to and from shopping centers, doctors, church, etc.	9.86	24.12	12.84	9.45
Directories of individuals willing to trade services	7.40	18.47	7.43	13.39
Special assistance phone numbers, with the operator helping in locating the nearest certified person available to provide a service (like repairs)	10.41	24.76	15.54	18.11
A medical ID card that can be electronically read by medical staff in case of emergency to show them useful information (like conditions, allergies, doctors, and medications)	33.70	61.41	52.03	44.88
Directories of numbers which you can call to get prerecorded information on various topics, such as special events, store sales, vacation packages, and financial and medical news	13.70	22.51	11.49	21.26

dulgers than to healthy hermits, while about twice as many ailing outgoers as healthy hermits and frail recluses showed interest in joining a club that provides a variety of services.

Four in ten older Americans labeled as "ailing outgoers" indicated high probability of using a personal health-alarm system. This compares with one in six healthy hermits and a little over one in four for the remaining groups. Ailing outgoers and healthy indulgers were also more likely to express interest in using a home-alarm system than the remaining groups. About four in ten in these two groups indicated definite or probable use of this product, in comparison with 26 percent of frail recluses and 25 percent of healthy hermits. A larger percentage of ailing outgoers and frail recluses than healthy hermits would buy products demonstrated on TV via home computer or telephone. About one in four ailing outgoers, in comparison with about one in ten older adults in the remaining gerontographic groups, are interested in using community vans. Directories of individuals willing to trade services are also of greater interest to ailing outgoers than to healthy hermits and frail recluses. Nearly one in four ailing outgoers, in comparison with one in ten healthy hermits, 16 percent of frail recluses, and 18 percent of healthy indulgers, are interested in special-assistance phone numbers. Nearly twice as many ailing outgoers as healthy hermits would use a medical ID card containing medical information, with about half of the frail recluses and 45 percent of healthy indulgers indicating usage likelihood. Finally, audiotext is likely to have greater appeal to ailing outgoers and healthy indulgers than to the remaining groups.

In sum, differences in responses across gerontographic groups were noted for all thirteen products examined. These findings further suggest the value of using gerontographic characteristics in predicting the older person's likelihood of purchasing new products and services.

SUMMARY AND IMPLICATIONS

The results of the research presented run contrary to conventional wisdom that older adults are technology averse. Many technological innovations have less value to older consumers than they do to younger consumers because of differences in lifestyles. Technologies that provide obvious benefits to older adults are likely to be welcome. Therefore, it is imperative for marketers who develop new technology-based products for the older population to communicate the significant benefits of the innovations and to properly position these products. Research also suggests that new products, especially technological innovations, be positioned in line with the older person's needs (perceived product benefits). The new product's benefits need to be made obvious to the mature person by emphasizing how it can satisfy older consumer needs for independence, security, sociability, and other relevant needs the product/service might satisfy (see Chapter 3). In addition, emphasis needs to be placed on making the product or service "user-friendly." Marketers must take into consideration the older person's declining cognitive abilities, fears, and reluctance to learn about new products, and they should try to present innovations as simply as possible. One strategy for achieving this objective is to relate the new innovation to an existing one the older consumer already uses. For example, directions for using new electronic appliances, such as microwave ovens, should be similar to those applicable to existing appliances. Another strategy for marketers in introducing new products is to appeal to the older consumer's younger relatives who would be in a better position to explain the product's benefits and operation procedures to the older person.

One of the interesting findings of this research is that many of the products expected to appeal to older persons are of equal or even greater appeal to younger adults. This suggests the need to avoid marketing new products exclusively to older consumers. Such strategies might not only keep potential younger buyers away but could also alienate the mature market. Again, stressing product functionality and benefits appears to be the most viable approach to marketing new products.

The data presented in this chapter help us develop profiles of older adults who have favorable attitudes toward technologies, actually use recently introduced technologies, and intend to use new/emerging products and technologies. Older adults who favor new technologies are most likely to be younger, male, and live in northern and western states; they are most likely to be struggling full-nesters and least likely to be healthy hermits. Owners and users of recent technologies are also likely to be owners and users of other technologies. While sociodemographic, lifestyle, and gerontographic characteristics relate to a number of new or emerging innovations, there is no consistent pattern of relationship between specific characteristics and various innovations. This suggests the need to develop profiles of specific innovations, rather than assume that potential adopters of these have similar sociodemographic and lifestyle profiles.

9

Distribution Decisions

Marketing decisions must be made with respect to a wide variety of areas of product distribution. First, a product or service can be distributed via different methods (e.g., direct, through retailers). Second, after choosing a specific method, several subdecisions must be made. For example, direct distribution involves mail, phone, catalog, and "door-to-door" selling. Similarly, a product/service can be distributed through a variety of retail outlets, including discount, specialty, and department stores. Third, a wide variety of decisions that apply to a specific type of retail outlets must be made, such as decisions relating to merchandising, shelf space, store operations, and customer services.

When marketing products and services to the mature market, one must address a variety of issues: Should different emphasis be placed on different distribution methods when marketing to older consumers? Should different emphasis be placed on specific types of distribution methods such as direct (mail, phone, etc.) and retail (discount, specialty, department store)? Should retailers develop special retail strategies to appeal to the older population? If so, which elements of the retailing mix should be changed and how?

Answers to these questions require knowledge of the older person's responses to several retailing stimuli—that is, orientations toward retailing stimuli, as well as consumer needs and wants—but information is not always adequate to help decision makers. Furthermore, such orientations must be determined for older consumers possessing different characteristics, since it is widely known that the mature market is heterogeneous and older consumers are likely to behave differently on the basis of several demographic, psychological, and social characteristics. This chapter summarizes existing knowledge from previous studies, and the results of our study attempt to fill gaps in knowledge regarding the older person's orientations toward retailing stimuli.

METHODS OF DISTRIBUTION

Consumers have two main options of purchasing most products and services: in-store and nonstore. While the two methods are not mutually exclusive, direct buying is more likely to supplement in-store buying. Thus, of interest to marketers is the older consumer's orientations toward various methods of at-home or direct buying.

Although older people are likely to buy products and services at home, views usually vary when it comes to answering questions such as how much they buy, what they buy, what direct buying mode they prefer (phone, mail, door-to-door), and whether they buy more than younger adults. Older consumers appear to be willing to buy products at home, but they may not buy as frequently as their younger counterparts. This is because older people may not make as many purchases as younger consumers who are more likely to live in larger families and therefore have more needs for shopping as a result of their stage in life (such as full-nest working couples).

While some studies found limited in-home shopping activity by older adults, other studies do not confirm these data, suggesting that the shopping method may vary by type of product involved. A study by Goldring & Company (1987), for example, found clothing, books, seeds and plants, records and tapes, hobby and craft items, housewares, vitamins, and film developing to be the most popular mail-order items for the 50-and-over age group. Mail-order buying of clothing and accessories, housewares and cookware, and books or educational materials has also been found to be most common among adults between the ages of 55 and 65 (Moschis 1992b). Again, we seem to know little about the reasons these differences in preference relate to age groups, but it is likely that they may derive from changes that occur in age-related needs and motivations in late stages of life.

PREFERENCE FOR TYPES OF OUTLETS

The type of store preferred by older consumers varies by type of purchase. One study of clothing-buying behavior found that 62 percent of older shoppers patronized major department stores, compared with 12 percent for specialty stores, catalog/mail order, and discount stores (Schutz, Baird, and Hawkes, 1979). For home furnishings, on the other hand, furniture stores were preferred by 52 percent of the 50-plus group, compared with 20 and 18 percent for department stores and specialty stores, respectively, according to another study reported in *American Demographics* (1988).

Preferences for retail outlets vary not only by type of store but by age as well. Research shows that older shoppers, in comparison to their younger counterparts, prefer shopping at department stores rather than discount stores, and they prefer specialty stores more than discount stores (Moschis 1992b).

Older consumers appear to be loyal shoppers, more so than their younger counterparts, Jo-Ann Zbytniewski (1979) reported higher degrees of loyalty to food stores among older adults than among younger shoppers. Other studies also showed high degrees of loyalty to stores among older consumers. Higher loyalty to stores by older adults may be partly explained by the mature person's lower propensity to move to other locations (older adults are about four times less likely to move than younger adults) (Moschis 1992b).

PATRONAGE REASONS

Mature consumers use a variety of criteria in choosing among stores, but services offered appear to be of primary importance (Mason and Bearden 1978). Such services include courteous, patient treatment by store employes; assistance in locating products; transportation to and from shopping area; and places to rest when they become tired (Moschis 1992b). Similarly, other studies suggest that special treatment (such as carry-out service for packages), special considerations (such as assistance in product selection), and similar-aged clerks affect the mature person's patronage habits (Schewe 1984). The importance of such services increases with the age of the older consumer (Lumpkin, Greenberg, and Goldstucker 1985). Desire for these services might indeed reflect cognitive and biological changes (such as information-processing skills and immobility) due to aging.

Although mature consumers use criteria similar to those used by younger consumers in evaluating and selecting retail outlets, the importance of these criteria varies not only with age but also with type of outlet and purpose of the shopping trip (Moschis 1992b). For example, personal assistance and ease of returning merchandise appear to be important reasons for patronizing clothing and shoe stores; cleanliness and clearly marked prices are important in patronizing food stores; and location, personnel/staff, and fees are important in selecting a hospital.

NEW INSIGHTS

Our study sought to enhance our knowledge in this area; it investigated various types of orientations toward retail outlets, including direct mar-

Table 9.1
Orientations Toward Retail Outlets

	Strongly/ Somewhat Disagree %	Neither Agree Nor Disagree %	Strongly/ Somewhat Agree %
Store Loyalty			
I prefer doing most of my shopping in the same stores I have always shopped in	11.4	17.1	71.5
I would rather buy several services (like financial and insurance) from one place than deal with a different company for each service	18.8	15.0	66.3
I judge the value of some products by the name of the store that sells them	27.6	22.8	49.6
Service			
I would be interested in having a personal adviser at places where I buy products and services whom I could call for assistance or complaints	24.9	32.3	42.8
Stores should have valet parking for those customers who need it	34.2	37.6	28.2
I would not buy a new product unless I knew it would be easy to return	15.0	24.5	60.5
Location			
I do not mind paying higher prices if a store is conveniently located	37.2	20.4	42.3
Direct Marketing Methods			
I often buy products or services by phone	68.3	15.8	15.9
I often order items from catalogs or magazines	47.5	15.8	36.7

Note: Row percentage figures may not add up to 100.0 due to rounding off.

keting methods, store loyalty, store location, and various forms of services provided by stores. These orientations were assessed by asking respondents to indicate their level of agreement or disagreement with various types of statements designed to assess such orientations. Table 9.1 shows responses to these statements by those 55 years of age or older.

Direct marketing has been a topic of much dispute when it comes to older adults. While some studies have found low use of direct marketing methods, others have shown a higher percentage of older adults using them. In our survey we asked respondents to agree or disagree with two specific statements: "I often buy products or services by phone" and "I often order items from catalogs or magazines." Only 16 percent of those 55 and older agreed to the first statement, with the majority of them disagreeing with the statement. A little over one-third of the respondents admitted to frequently ordering items from catalogs or magazines, with the majority of them again disagreeing. These responses compare very favorably with those reported by James R. Lumpkin, Marjorie J. Caballero, and Lawrence B. Chonko (1987) who found 15 percent and 35 percent of older adults using direct mail and catalogues, respectively. However, it should be noted that Lumpkin, Caballero, and Chonko's study questioned those 65 and older with respect to their purchases in the previous six months.

Mature adults have favorable orientations toward stores. Specifically, they tend to be loyal to certain stores. Older Americans prefer to patronize the same stores rather than switching retail outlets. More than 70 percent of our older respondents expressed preference for doing most of their shopping in the same stores they have always shopped in. Two-thirds of the mature adults surveyed indicated preference for purchasing related services from the same service provider over dealing with a different company for each service. Finally, older adults are likely to use the store name in evaluating products and services; nearly half of the respondents indicated a tendency to judge the value of some products by the name of the store that sells them.

Older Americans appear to value several types of services offered by retail outlets. When asked about the desirability of having a personal adviser whom they could call for assistance, the largest majority was in favor of this ideas. However, this was not the case for valet parking. Although a large percentage favored this service, the majority of the respondents did not find this type of service desirable. Finally, a liberal return policy appears to be valued by older consumers. Three of five older adults questioned indicated that they would not buy a new product unless they knew it would be easy to return it, while only 15 percent did not feel that ability to return products was a major concern. Many older Americans value store location to the point that they would not hesitate paying higher prices for its products. Over 40 percent would sacrifice higher prices for location, in comparison to 37 percent of the older Americans who would not.

Older versus Younger Shoppers' Opinions

In order to put these responses in perspective, responses given by older adults were compared to those given by younger adults. The results are shown in Table 9.2.

It is interesting to note that the two age groups differed very little when they were asked about their direct marketing preferences. Almost as many

Table 9.2
Orientations Toward Retail Outlets among Younger (under 55) and Older (55+) Adults (percentage "strongly/somewhat agree")

	Younger	Older
Store Loyalty		
I prefer doing most of my shopping in the same stores I have always shopped in	64.4	71.6
I would rather buy several services (like financial and insurance) from one place than deal with a different company for each service	59.1	66.7
I judge the value of some products by the name of the store that sells them	42.5	49.1
Service		
I would be interested in having a personal adviser at places where I buy products and services whom I could call for assistance or complaints	38.7	42.2
Stores should have valet parking for those customers who need it	21.5	28.4
I would not buy a new product unless I knew it would be easy to return	51.8	60.7
Location		
I do not mind paying higher prices if a store is conveniently located	38.1	44.1
Direct Marketing Methods		
I often buy products or services by phone	15.6	15.8
I often order items from catalogs or magazines	39.7	36.5

older adults as younger adults buy products by phone and from catalogs or magazines.

There are several age-related differences in orientations toward retail facilities that deserve attention. First, with respect to store loyalty, older adults appear to prefer patronizing the same stories, more so than their younger counterparts. Similarly, a larger percentage of older consumers expressed preference for purchasing several services from the same service provider, in comparison to younger adults. Finally, older adults expressed a greater trust than those under 55 years of age in the name of certain stores. All these data appear to suggest a more favorable orientation toward retail outlets among older than among younger Americans.

Responses given to present and hypothetical store services were also compared between the two age groups. A larger percentage of older adults expressed preference for having a personal adviser for assistance and complaints in places where they shop. Similarly, valet parking is more preferred by older than younger shoppers, with 28 percent and 21 percent expressing preference, respectively. Finally, older consumers again were found to be more favorably oriented toward a liberal return policy, with 61 percent of them, in comparison to 52 percent of their younger counterparts, expressing a favorable orientation.

Locational convenience is also valued more by older adults. Forty-four percent of those 55 and older indicated willingness to pay higher prices for locational convenience, in comparison with 38 percent of younger adults. However, since the response to the statement applies to location in relation to price, this response would mean either a stronger orientation toward location or lower significance of price in the purchasing process.

Sociodemographic Influences

Preferences for direct marketing methods show relatively little variability in late life. There appears to be a slight increase in shopping by phone, catalogs, or magazines among those in the 65-to-74 age bracket in comparison to those in the younger group. The use of these methods shows a slight (and statistically insignificant) decline among the oldest group. This might be due to physical limitations or even constriction of needs for products and services among the very old.

One of our interests in this research was the examination of the extent to which orientations toward retail outlets vary by select sociodemographic characteristics. Thus, our analysis also included the comparison of responses among respondents of different age groups (55-64, 65-74, 75+), sex, geographic location, and income.

Although there is a slight increase with age in the older person's propensity to express a stronger preference for shopping in the same store, the increase is negligible. The same appears to be the case with preference for buying similar services from the same place. However, when it comes to judging the value of products by the name of the store that sells them, the 65-and-older groups show a higher tendency to do so than their younger counterparts.

Services offered by stores are likely to be perceived as more valuable by the oldest group (75+). When asked to indicate their interest in having a personal adviser at places where they buy products and services, more than half of those 75 or older indicated preference, in comparison with 41 percent among those 55 to 64 years of age. Similarly, the need for valet parking increases with age; while 23 percent of the youngest group agreed with the statement "Stores should have valet parking for those customers who need it," the percentage was about twice as large among those 75 years of age or older. Finally, there was a similar increase with age with respect to preference for a liberal return policy; while 58 percent of those aged 55 to 64 indicated preference, 65 percent of those over 75 did the same. Thus, store services appear to become increasingly important with age.

The importance of locational convenience also increases with age. While 39 percent of those age 55 to 64 reported preference for convenient location at a higher price, 51 percent of the oldest group expressed a similar response.

Certain orientations toward stores show interesting variations with age within select income categories. With respect to patterns of store loyalty, the tendency to prefer several services from the same source increases with age only among upper-income older adults (age 55+). Similarly, the inclination to judge the value of some products by the name of the store that sells them is especially influenced by age for the lower-income and upper-income brackets. Interest in having a personal adviser in retail outlets increases with age in late life among the lower-income respondents, remains constant among those in the middle-income bracket, and declines among those in the upper-income category. A somewhat similar pattern exists with respect to interest in valet parking. On the other hand, ease of returning merchandise becomes a relatively more important consideration with age among those in lower-income brackets than among those in upper-income brackets.

Age-related differences in responses among those 55 years of age or older were also assessed by taking into consideration the possible effects of a host of other factors that are related to age. This analysis revealed some interesting findings. One finding was that store loyalty tends to change little with age. Only the inclination to judge products by the name of the store that sells them increases with advancing age in late life. These findings suggest that other factors associated with age, not age per se, may be responsible for the observed favorable orientations toward retail outlets.

Orientations toward services remain the same when the effects of other factors such as sex, income, and education are taken into account. Only preferences for liberal return policy show no significant change in late life. The desire for locational convenience steadily increases with age. Also, the propensity to buy by phone shows a surprising increase with age, while the tendency to buy via catalogs and magazines changes very little. These findings collectively suggest that age itself maybe a surrogate factor representing several other characteristics (e.g., gender imbalance, education, income, mass media consumption). When these factors are taken into account along with age, the effects of age tend to be eliminated or canceled out. The analysis further suggests the danger of overrelying on age as an explanatory factor of the observed differences in consumer behavior in late life.

Some gender-related variations in orientations toward retail outlets were found. Specifically, male mature adults were found to be only marginally more inclined than their female counterparts to agree with the statement "I judge the value of some products by the name of the store that sells them" (51.1% versus 47.7%). Males were also more inclined than their female counterparts to express interest in having a personal adviser at places where they shop to help them with various shopping-related activities (46.0% versus 39.9%). No other significant variation in response due to sex was noted.

Responses were also analyzed by geographic region (east, north, south and west; see page 66 for methodology). There are several interesting differences. A larger portion of southerners (40.1%) and easterners (39.0%) are more likely to order items from catalogs or magazines than older adults living in western states (31.8%). With respect to store loyalty, as indicated by the responses given to the statement "I prefer doing most of my shopping in the same store I have always shopped in," mature adults from southern states are the least loyal (65.2%), while westerners are the most loyal shoppers (76.0%). However, westerners are less likely to buy several services from the same source (60.5%) in comparison to those older adults living in northern states (68.7%). The types of services preferred by older respondents appear to vary a great deal based on geographic location. Regarding their interest in having a personal shopping adviser, mature respondents living in eastern states showed preference about 50 percent stronger than that expressed by older Americans in the remaining geographic groups. Southerners, on the other hand, expressed a stronger preference for valet parking than older Americans living in the west (32.8% versus 21.9%). Finally, ability to return merchandise is more important among those living in the east (65.8%) than among those in the west (52.5%). There are also geographic variations with respect to locational convenience, with a larger percentage of southerners (47.4%) reporting such preference than their westerner counterparts (37.4%).

Another concern in our study was the examination of orientations toward retail facilities by specific level of income of older adults. It was expected that income may serve as an enabling or constraining factor in older adults' store orientations as assessed by the responses to various types of statements. Responses to direct marketing showed very little variability with income. Thus, having more money available does not necessarily translate into greater use of direct marketing channels of distribution. Store loyalty is lower among those older adults with incomes in excess of $50,000, in comparison to their lower-income counterparts. Similar differences exist with respect to preferences for buying several services from one location/facility. For example, while 69 percent of those older respondents with annual incomes less than $30,000 expressed interest in buying several services from one place rather than deal with a different company for each service, 53 percent of those with an income of $50,000 or greater gave a similar response. The desirability of various services declines somewhat with income. For example, while 44 percent of older adults with incomes under $30,000 expressed interest in having a personal adviser to assist them in stores, the percentage of those with incomes $50,000 or more who want this service is smaller (38.8%). Similarly, the lower-income group differs from the upper-income group in its preferences for valet parking (31.9% versus 20.1%). A liberal return policy is also preferred more by those with lower incomes (62.5%) than by those with higher incomes (52.8%). Locational convenience at a higher price, on the other hand, increases in importance with higher income. Among those with less than $30,000 in annual income, 38 percent agreed with the statement "I do not mind paying higher prices if a store is conveniently located," compared with 49 percent of those with incomes $50,000 or more.

Shopping Orientations of Need-Based Clusters

Consumer needs and consumption-related concerns were also expected to translate into different orientations toward retail outlets. To examine the relationship between these needs and orientations toward retail outlets, responses given to statements tapping these orientations were analyzed by need-based clusters.

Some variations in preference and use of direct marketing methods can be seen across the four clusters, especially between self-sufficients and struggling full-nesters, with the former group being more likely to report purchasing products or services by phone (16.6%) than the latter group (9.8%). Although a similar difference in responses exists with respect to the use of catalogs or magazines as sources of direct buying, this percentage is not statistically significant.

Struggling full-nesters are most likely to express preference for patronizing the same stores (store loyalty), with more than three-fourths (77.2%) of the respondents in this group providing affirmative responses, in comparison with less than two-thirds (64.9%) of young insecureds. Struggling full-nesters are also more likely than respondents in other need-based clusters, especially the dependent frail, to express a strong preference for purchasing related services from the same service provider (69.9% versus 59.7%, respectively).

Preferences for various types of services show slight variation across need-based clusters. The only noticeable difference is with regard to preference for a liberal return policy where a larger percentage of self-sufficients value this service, in comparison with older adults classified as young insecureds (56.2%) and struggling full-nesters (56.9%). Locational convenience is a factor of greater importance among young insecureds

Table 9.3
Orientations Toward Retail Outlets by Gerontographic Clusters (percentage "strongly/somewhat agree")

	Healthy Hermits	Ailing Outgoers	Frail Recluses	Healthy Indulgers
Store Loyalty				
I prefer doing most of my shopping in the same store I have always shopped in	70.96	70.42	72.30	67.72
I would rather buy several services (like financial and insurance) from one place than deal with a different company for each service	57.81	68.81	65.54	66.93
I judge the value of some products by the name of the store that sells them	49.86	49.52	52.03	50.39
Service				
I would be interested in having a personal adviser at places where I buy products or services, whom I could call for assistance or complaints	39.18	51.13	45.27	40.94
Stores should have valet parking for those customers who need it	20.55	34.73	30.41	27.56
I would not buy a new product unless I knew it would be easy to return	55.89	64.95	62.84	62.20
Location				
I do not mind paying higher prices if a store is conveniently located	41.92	44.31	41.98	38.58
Direct Marketing Methods				
I often buy products or services by phone	13.15	15.76	15.54	15.75
I often order items from catalogs or magazines	33.97	36.66	38.51	33.07

(44.9%) and dependent frail (45.9%) than among struggling full-nesters (35.8%).

Orientations by Gerontographic Clusters

Various orientations toward stores by gerontographic clusters are shown in Table 9.3. Responses to methods of direct buying did not vary much among gerontographic clusters. While there were few variations in preferences for shopping in the same stores among older adults across the four gerontographic clusters, responses by healthy hermits and ailing outgoers were the two extremes in assessing older adults' preferences for "one-stop shopping" for various services. Although percentages are on the affirmative side, the former group is the least concerned while the latter is the most concerned.

When it comes to preferences for various services, ailing outgoers are the most demanding of all gerontographic groups. A little over half of them expressed interest in having a personal adviser who would assist them in retail outlets, in comparison with 39 percent of healthy hermits and 41 percent of healthy indulgers. Similarly, a little over one-third of ailing outgoers, in comparison with 21 percent of healthy hermits, expressed interest in valet parking. Finally, nearly as many ailing outgoers as frail recluses expressed a positive orientation toward a liberal return policy.

Location was almost equally valued by older adults in the gerontographic groups, although ailing outgoers were somewhat more likely than healthy indulgers to favor locational convenience over price.

IMPLICATIONS FOR RETAILERS

The data presented here suggest that older consumers are not likely to respond to distribution strategies and stimuli in a uniform fashion. Rather, such responses are likely to be the result of several characteristics of mature consumers. Thus, based on the results of the information presented in this chapter, one can develop a profile of individuals who are most likely to respond favorably to various distribution methods, types of retail establishments, and specific retail stimuli.

Direct marketing methods are likely to be most effective when they are directed at older consumers who have the following characteristics:

- age 65 to 74
- live in southern and eastern states
- live in rural areas
- belong to "self-sufficient" need-based cluster

Older Americans who are *loyal to stores* tend to have the following characteristics:

- live in western states
- have lower income (under $50,000)
- are most likely to belong to "struggling full-nester" need-based group

Mature Americans who favor *one-stop-shopping*, and therefore may favor obtaining products and services from nontraditional product/service providers, tend to have the following characteristics:

- live in northern states
- have household income of less than $50,000
- belong to "struggling full-nesters" need-based group
- are likely to belong to "ailing outgoers" gerontographic group

Those who are most likely to place *trust in the name of a store* are:

- 65 or older
- male

The availability of a *personal adviser* is of greatest appeal to older adults who are:

- 75 and older
- male
- most likely to live in eastern states
- most likely to have income under $30,000
- most likely to be "ailing outgoers"

The most likely to respond favorably to *valet parking*:

- are 75 and older
- live in southern states

Mature consumers who are most likely to be attracted to a marketer's *liberal return policy* tend to have the following characteristics:

- are 75 and older
- live in eastern states
- have low income
- are most likely to belong to "self-sufficients" need-based group
- are most likely to be "ailing outgoers"

Finally, older Americans who value *locational convenience* are likely to have the following profile:

- are older
- live in the south
- have higher income
- belong to "young insecureds" or "dependent frail" need-based clusters

The research presented in this chapter has several implications for retailers. The emerging themes from the studies highlight the importance of convenience in the minds of older adults. While some types of shopping may be a form of entertainment and present opportunities for socialization, in most occasions older adults appear to seek ways to make shopping less difficult and more convenient. In late life, several services are especially valued; most notable are personal service and assistance with completing the shopping task. Therefore, retailers are advised to emphasize the convenience aspect in their promotional strategy or to create retail environments that make shopping easy and pleasant.

The older person's inclination to prefer "one-stop shopping" with increasing age suggests the value of a marketing strategy that involves placing several diverse departments within a store. For example, the recent trend toward placing pharmacies in supermarkets is consistent with the older person's desire for convenience. Similarly, locating a store near other types of stores would serve the same purpose. Finally, the findings highlight the value of gerontographic segmentation in designing retail strategy.

10

Designing the Promotional Mix

Promotion is a broad area of marketing activities and includes advertising, personal selling, and sales promotion. The last category includes a number of price-saving incentives and "free" gifts. Many types of price reductions such as coupons, rebates, and even "sales" specials can be classified under sales promotion. How effective are the various sales promotion activities in marketing to older consumers? This chapter reviews previous research studies that have attempted to assess older persons' responses to various sales promotion strategies and presents the results of a large-scale national study designed to enhance our understanding in this area. These research findings are used, in turn, to suggest implications for developing effective promotional strategies to appeal to older consumers.

Several studies have examined older persons' responses to different sales promotion tactics. A survey by the Roper Organization examined how older shoppers (age 60 and older) respond to a number of sales promotion strategies in relation to their younger counterparts (age 45 to 59). Generally, respondents in both age groups responded the same way to samples (at the store and in the mail), coupons, gifts with purchases, and free trial examination of products. However, older adults were less likely than younger consumers to respond to frequent-use program offerings (such as frequent flier programs) and to store catalogs they receive in the mail (Gross 1989). Sweepstakes were found to have minimum influence on purchasing decision of shoppers regardless of age, according to a Donnelley Marketing study (Balkite 1988). Price is always an important consideration in almost any purchasing decision, especially among older consumers. A Food Marketing Institute study (Miklos 1982), for example, found that older adults look for store specials more than any other age group. However, the importance of price as a criterion in decision making tends to vary by type of purchase situation (Miklos 1982). A study of 715 adults age 55 and older conducted by the Center for Mature Consumers Studies (CMCS) found that price becomes increasingly important as the value or quality of the product or service becomes standardized (Moschis 1992b). When product quality or performance varies, price is likely to play a secondary role. Generally, quality is believed to be far more important than price among older adults.

Survey data also suggest that older people are inclined to switch brands if offered certain money-saving incentives. According to a survey by Donnelley Marketing, 44 percent of Americans age 50 and over could be persuaded to switch brands through cents-off coupons, with 84 percent of them indicating usage of coupons once or more monthly, and 17 percent of them using coupons once a week (*Marketing News* 1987). However, the Donnelley study did not compare older adults' coupon usage to that of younger adults.

The importance of various types of promotional stimuli appears to depend on the type of product or service purchased. Senior discounts appear to be of greatest importance in deciding on brands of drugs and health aids. According to a CMCS study, about three-fourths (78%) of the respondents indicated senior discounts are important in choosing over-the-counter (OTC) drugs and health aids (Moschis 1992b). In the same study, coupons were found to be nearly twice as important to older consumers as any other brand attribute in choosing among brands of food and alcoholic beverages, with 66 percent of the respondents indicating their importance. While money-saving incentives such as cents-off coupons appear to be a major consideration in buying grocery products, other incentives tend to be ignored by select segments of the older population. For example, studies have consistently found low use of food stamps by older adults, although many of them are eligible for this type of assistance (Moschis and Payne 1991). Low utilization of food stamps has been attributed to a number of factors including (1) difficulty in obtaining the stamps (requiring monthly trips to the food stamp office) and (2) stigmatization of the elderly in a public setting as being recipients of charity or public largess. Another reason for the low food-stamp usage reported by older adults may be that many of those who apply never receive them.

Money-saving incentives appear to be most effective when they are offered on private (store) brands rather than on national (manufacturer) brands. A study by J. Barry Mason and William O. Bearden (1978) revealed that the main reason older adults buy store brands is lower price, with about two-thirds of them citing this reason. Obviously, older adults do not believe that store brands are of the same or better quality, since only 12 percent indicated this to be the case in Mason and Bearden's study. However, more recent research by the Yankelovich Monitor, a market tracking service, showed that while preference for store brand names varies little with age, older women are more likely than older men to prefer store brands of food products (*American Demographics* 1991).

To summarize the results of previous research, while older adults appear to respond favorably to certain sales promotion stimuli, there is little evidence to suggest that they do so more than younger adults. Responses to specific sales promotion stimuli appear to be a matter of type of product or service purchased, and they may be influenced by certain consumer characteristics.

NEW INSIGHTS

Older-adult responses to variety of promotional practices were also assessed in our study. Specifically, our respondents were asked to give answers to a number of statements designed to assess their response to a variety of money-saving incentives, product samples, advertisements, salespeople, and in-store displays. The results of the responses given by those 55 years of age or older are shown in Table 10.1.

Money-Saving Incentives

Older adults appear to respond very favorably to money-saving incentives. Specifically, our survey sought to uncover orientations toward sales and coupons. With respect to special sales, respondents were asked to agree or disagree with three statements. One was aimed at uncovering in-store brand evaluation on the basis of special sales. Another was aimed at assessing out-of-store brand evaluation through advertisements of products on sales. The last statement was aimed at assessing impulse buying as a result of a sale.

Sixty-three percent of respondents indicated in-store brand evaluation based on price reduction. Similarly, about three-fourths of our sample said they usually watch the advertisements for announcement of sales, while about half admitted unplanned purchasing of brands due to a special sale.

Survey participants were also asked to respond to two statements designed to tap their orientations toward use of coupons. Again, nearly three-fourths of our respondents expressed agreement with the statement "I use coupons with my purchases, whenever I can." Similarly, the majority of the respondents agreed that a special sale or coupon will tempt them to buy a different brand from the one they usually buy.

These data collectively suggest strong orientations toward "specials." However, a major portion of older adults appear to use these "deals" to buy brands they already prefer or customarily buy rather than switch to new or different brands.

Table 10.1
Responses to Promotional Practices

	Strongly/ Somewhat Disagree %	Neither Agree Nor Disagree %	Strongly/ Somewhat Agree %
Money-Saving Incentives			
Before I decide which brand to buy, I check to see which brands are on sale	19.9	17.1	63.0
I usually watch the advertisements for announcement of sales	10.8	12.6	76.6
A special sale will tempt me to buy an item I hadn't planned on buying	36.0	14.3	49.6
I use coupons with my purchases, whenever I can	15.4	10.7	73.9
A special sale or coupon will tempt me to buy a different brand from the one I usually buy	26.1	16.8	57.1
Samples			
I would hesitate buying a new health care product if I have not used a free sample of it	22.4	29.6	48.0
Advertisements			
I have bought products/services because I liked their ads	38.3	29.5	32.2
Salespeople			
When I go shopping, I often ask salespeople to help me buy things for myself	62.3	22.3	15.4
In-Store Displays			
I am attracted to special displays in a store	32.3	31.2	36.6

Samples

Product samples appear to be an effective way to introduce new products into the market. Nearly half of our older sample agreed with the statement "I would hesitate buying a new health care product, if I have not used a free sample of it."

Advertisements

One statement was used to assess responses to advertisements. Specifically, respondents were asked to tell us if they had bought products and services because they liked their ads. Nearly one in three older adults admitted having bought products/services because of their ads; a somewhat larger percent disagreed, while nearly 30 percent expressed no opinion.

Salespeople

Salespeople received low scores as a source of advice and help in buying products. Only 15 percent of older adults admitted asking salespeople for advice when buying products for themselves; 62 percent gave a negative response, while 22 percent gave a neutral answer.

In-Store Displays

Finally, we asked our respondents to provide agree-disagree responses to the statement "I am attracted to special displays in a store." Responses to this statement were roughly equally distributed, with a little over one-third of the older adults providing affirmative responses and a little under one-third providing either negative responses or no strong opinion.

Responses by Age

Older adults' (55 and over) responses to various promotional practices were also compared to those given by younger adults (under 55) (Table 10.2). With respect to money-saving incentives, older adults indicated a higher propensity to evaluate brands based on special sales and to watch advertisements for announcement of sales. Older adults also tend to use coupons whenever they can, more so than their younger counterparts. However, coupons are not likely to result in unplanned purchases as much for older adults as they are for younger shoppers.

Older adults responded very favorably to product samples. While nearly half of them admitted using free samples for health products, only about one-third of the younger adults indicated trial use via free samples. These differences may also reflect differences in usage rates of health products by the two age groups. The remaining promotional practices are perceived about equally by both younger and older adults.

Thus, contrary to the results of previous studies, our research suggests that older adults have more favorable orientations toward money-saving incentives than their younger counterparts. They are also more receptive to free samples, suggesting that product sampling might be used to reduce risk perceived in the purchase of a new product. While many other sales promotion offerings appear to be perceived favorably by the older market, their importance is roughly equal to that of younger consumers.

Table 10.2
Responses to Promotional Practices among Younger (under 55) and Older
(55+) Adults (percentage "strongly/somewhat agree")

	Younger	Older
Money-Saving Incentives		
Before I decide which brand to buy, I check to see which brands are on sale	41.2	62.5
I usually watch the advertisements for announcement of sales	68.1	76.0
A special sale will tempt me to buy an item I hadn't planned on buying	52.7	49.0
I use coupons with my purchases, whenever I can	62.3	71.9
A special sale or coupon will tempt me to buy a different brand from the one I usually buy	63.2	55.9
Samples		
I would hesitate buying a new health care product if I have not used a free sample of it	34.9	46.4
Advertisements		
I have bought products/services because I liked their ads	34.4	31.6
Salespeople		
When I go shopping, I often ask salespeople to help me buy things for myself	12.4	15.9
In-Store Displays		
I am attracted to special displays in a store	36.3	36.3

Sociodemographic Differences

Answers to questions regarding promotional practices were also assessed by other sociodemographic attributes, including specific age groups of older adults. Responses were categorized into three groups: 55–64, 65–74, and 75 or older. This analysis suggested that the propensity to buy whatever brand is on sale increases somewhat with age. The very old in particular are more likely to engage in unplanned purchasing when items are on sale. on the other hand, use of coupons remains relatively stable with age. Responses to free samples appear to be more favorable among the older age groups, and so are responses to advertisements. People become increasingly dependent on salespeople for assistance in buying as they get older, while self-reported responses to in-store displays remain relatively constant. Many of these findings were also confirmed when more rigorous analysis was done. Specifically, when we considered the possible effects of age-related factors (such as education, income, sex, etc.), the findings about the effects of age on responses to sales and coupons remain the same and so does the respondents' inclination to use samples, advertisements, and salespeople's help.

Orientations toward money-saving incentives become increasingly stronger with age particularly among middle-income adults. However, this observation can only be made on select brands and items ordinarily purchased and does not apply to unplanned purchasing behavior. "Specials" become more effective in inducing unplanned purchases with age among those older adults in upper-income groups. Money-saving incentives as a means of brand switching (most likely to other "acceptable" brands) are most effective among those in middle- and upper-income brackets. Finally, in-store displays appear to become increasingly effective with age only among the middle-income older adults.

Differences in responses by sex were also examined. It was expected that the gender of older adults would affect their responses to various promotional practices due to different experiences as shoppers as well as due to different sex roles experienced earlier in life. The results of this analysis suggested that the propensity to engage in unplanned purchases due to special sales tends to be higher among females than among males, with 54 percent and 42 percent, respectively, agreeing that special sales often tempt them to buy something they had not planned on buying. The same appeared to be the case with respect to the use of coupons. Finally, free samples appear to be more favorably received by females than males, with a little over half (52%) of the former group agreeing that they would hesitate purchasing a health product without first trying a free sample, compared with 42 percent of males. This suggests that females may be more risk averse than their male counterparts.

Because we had no specific expectations with respect to "what" or "why" geographic differences should exist, our analysis was simply exploratory. Agreement responses to various statements related to promotional practices were tabulated by region (east, north, south, and west). While easterners are most likely to engage in unplanned buying, especially in comparison to those older adults living in southern states (63.9% versus 53.9%, respectively), they are also the group least likely to report brand switching as a result of a special sale or coupon. Easterners are also more likely than their southerner counterparts to value free samples, with 52 percent of those in the former group and 43 percent of the latter group providing positive responses. Finally, easterners are more likely than southerners to buy products/services because they like their ads (37.1%

versus 29.2%) and to report attraction to special in-store displays (40.9% versus 32.4%).

Responses were analyzed by income. Older respondents were grouped into three categories based on household income (under $30,000; $30,000–$49,999; and $50,000 or more). The analysis showed that older persons' propensity to respond to sales and coupons declines with increasing income. Thus, older adults with high income are not as likely as low-income older Americans to be attracted to money-saving incentives. The same appears to be the case with free samples, while responses to advertisements are more positive among the middle-income older adults (36.8%) than among those in the lower-income bracket (28.8%). On the other hand, the lower-income older adults are nearly twice as likely as their middle-income counterparts to ask for salespeople's assistance in buying products (18.5% versus 9.7%, respectively). Finally, those in the upper-income bracket are less likely to express attraction to special in-store displays than their middle-income counterparts (30.1% versus 38.3%).

Orientations by Need-Based Clusters

Some differences in responses were uncovered when tabulations were made according to need-based clusters. Deciding to buy brands on sale is more common among the dependent frail (63.8%) than among young insecureds (57.8%). Brands on sale are more likely to induce unplanned purchases among self- sufficients (48.3%) than among older adults in other need-based segments. The propensity to use coupons and buy products on sale on a regular basis, which results in brand switching, is generally higher among the self-sufficients than among struggling full-nesters. Young insecureds are slightly more likely to use free samples (47.6%) than the dependent frail groups (41.0%). Finally, in-store displays are of greater appeal to struggling full-nesters (38.2%) than to young insecureds (29.7%).

Responses by Gerontographic Groups

While responses did not vary greatly by need-based clusters, they did vary across the four gerontographic segments. Specifically, agreement responses provided by our older respondents were tallied by each gerontographic segment, as shown in Table 10.3.

The table shows that ailing outgoers are most likely to be receptive to various promotional stimuli. Ailing outgoers are more likely than healthy hermits to consider products on sale when selecting among brands of various products. They are also more likely to watch advertisements for announcements of sales than frail recluses and healthy indulgers, and they are more likely than healthy hermits to engage in unplanned purchases as a result of special sales. They are also more likely than healthy indulgers to use coupons with their purchases.

Table 10.3
Orientations Toward Promotional Practices by Gerontographic Clusters
(percentage "strongly/somewhat agree")

	Healthy Hermits	Ailing Outgoers	Frail Recluses	Healthy Indulgers
Money-Saving Incentives				
Before I decide which brand to buy, I check to see which brands are on sale	58.08	66.56	61.49	61.42
I usually watch the advertisements for announcements of sales	72.88	79.74	69.59	70.08
A special sale will tempt me to buy an item I hadn't planned on buying	41.92	49.84	47.97	43.31
I use coupons with my purchases, whenever I can	66.85	72.35	72.97	65.35
A special sale or coupon will tempt me to buy a different brand from the one I usually buy	53.70	54.66	50.68	51.97
Samples				
I would hesitate buying a new health care product if I have not used a free sample of it	37.53	56.27	42.57	35.43
Advertisements				
I have bought products/services because I liked their ads	32.33	32.80	28.38	33.86
Salespeople				
When I go shopping, I often ask salespeople to help me buy things for myself	12.60	20.26	16.22	18.90
In-Store Displays				
I am attracted to special displays in a store	29.32	38.91	32.43	42.52

Ailing outgoers are more likely than the remaining groups to use free samples and are also relatively more receptive to salespeople. Although this group is likely to be attracted to in-store displays, in comparison to healthy hermits, it is the healthy indulgers who show the greatest inclination to use in-store displays.

SUMMARY AND IMPLICATIONS

Older adults' responses to various promotional activities of business differ from those given by younger consumers. Furthermore, responses to specific promotional strategies are more positive among older adults possessing certain sociodemographic and gerontographic characteristics. While older shoppers are generally "deal prone," they are not likely to buy any brand just to save money; rather, they tend to confine their brand switching to familiar brands. Coupons appear to induce purchase of the same brand rather than to encourage brand switching.

The main implication of these findings for marketers and retailers is that the older consumer market needs to be segmented, and each segment should be approached with a different marketing strategy. While the majority of older adults may respond to promotional incentives by switching to familiar brands, some older consumers, especially those in lower-income brackets, would switch to less familiar brands. Thus, manufacturers contemplating branding strategies should keep in mind that a "family" branding strategy (same brand name for all products) might be more effective than an individual-name strategy. Money-saving incentives could be used by retailers to control store traffic more than store switching behavior. For example, midweek or early-day shopping specials are likely to appeal to older adults, helping retailers reduce store traffic during peak shopping times, as well as reducing overhead costs.

With respect to the issue of effectiveness of the various elements of the marketing mix, the research presented in this chapter suggests that the effectiveness of the various promotional tools may vary according to several characteristics of the older consumer segments. Based on existing knowledge and the results of the study presented, one can develop a profile of the older consumer who is most likely to respond favorably to the various promotional activities of the firm. Specifically, older consumers who tend to respond to various sales promotion strategies have unique profiles, depending upon the type of sales promotion stimulus. The demographic, lifestyle, and gerontographic profiles of older consumers who respond favorably to specific *sales promotion* stimuli can be summarized as follows:

Price Reduction/"Sale"

- very old (75+)
- females
- low income
- "dependent frail"
- "self-sufficients"
- "ailing outgoers"

Coupons

- low income
- "self-sufficients"

- "ailing outgoers"

Free Samples

- older (65+)
- low income
- "young insecureds"
- "ailing outgoers"

In-store Displays

- middle-income
- "struggling full-nesters"
- "healthy indulgers"

With respect to *advertising*, those most receptive to ads are likely to have the following characteristics:

- older (65+)
- middle income

Finally, older adults most likely to respond to *personal selling* efforts have the following characteristics:

- older
- low income
- "ailing outgoers"

Depending upon the characteristics of the target audience or segmentation basis marketers use, the effectiveness of various aspects of the promotional mix is likely to vary. For example, if one wishes to market to the very old, effective sales promotion mix should include money-saving incentives, free samples, advertising, and personal selling. On the other hand, if one targets ailing outgoers, a combination of money-saving incentives, free samples, coupons, and personal selling should be used.

11

Age-Targeted Marketing Strategies

With the emerging prominence of the mature market, several companies have begun to develop and promote products aimed at the aged population. While such products are aimed at satisfying specific needs of older consumers, the effectiveness of certain age-targeted marketing strategies has been the subject of controversy. For example, although hospitals and financial institutions have developed and promoted senior membership programs, many experts question the effectiveness of these programs. They argue that such programs are likely to offend many older people who psychologically deny the "old age" status. Critics of age-based marketing strategies cite examples that have failed such as Heinz baby food for older people (due to their difficulty with chewing hard foods) and Affinity shampoo for people with gray hair. Instead, they argue for intergenerational marketing strategies where the product is developed for (and promoted to) all age groups, stressing benefits of the product likely to be of interest to the older person.

How effective are these age-targeted marketing strategies? Are there any circumstances where these are likely to be most effective? The purpose of this chapter is to summarize existing knowledge on this topic and to present the results of our large-scale study designed to enhance our understanding.

RESPONSES TO AGE-TARGETED STRATEGIES

The effectiveness of age-targeted marketing strategies may vary depending upon who makes the assessment and the type of strategy under consideration. With respect to the source of assessment, evaluation of effectiveness can be provided by the marketer, the older consumer, and a third (independent) party such as a researcher. For the strategies under consideration, the main focus has been on three issues: (1) Should an older person be used as a spokesperson in an ad? If so, under what circumstances? (2) Should products be designed exclusively for older people, or should they be designed to appeal to several generations (intergenerational or "universal" design)? (3) How effective are various "age-membership" programs?

First, the age of the spokesperson in an ad is an issue. A survey of advertising executives found that the vast majority of advertising decision makers believe that older models in ads are effective in getting older consumers to respond in a favorable way (Greco 1988). Similarly, American Association of Retired Persons (AARP) guidelines recommend use of older spokespersons in advertisements. On the other hand, studies (Ward 1989; Milliman and Erffmeyer 1990) suggest that most older people do not identify with other older people in ads and that models should be chronologically younger (ten to fifteen years younger) than the average age of the intended target. Research also found that the elderly's responses to point-of-purchase advertising of an age-neutral product did not differ on the basis of the age of the models (Greco and Swayne 1992). This finding suggests that responses may differ only when the product is promoted exclusively to older adults. Thus, when older people know that the product is targeted exclusively at them, as in the case of arthritis pain relievers, they may try to defend their self-concept by identifying more with much younger spokespersons in advertisements. On the other hand, when the product (e.g., telecommunication services) appeals to a variety of age groups, older consumers may find the age of the spokesperson nonthreatening. For example, industry analysts have commented that telecommunication ads by several companies (e.g., AT&T featuring Cliff Robertson) have been very successful in appealing to the older population (Dychtwald and Flower 1989). This further suggests that older respondents may be more receptive to products that they do not perceive to be exclusively aimed at them, and they may avoid purchasing products designed for "older people" as a way of denying their old age.

While senior discount programs are popular in almost every industry, the available data point to mixed results. Peter L. Gillet and Robert L. Schneider (1978) reported that senior discount programs have marginally positive effects. Zarrel V. Lambert found that nearly half (53%) of Florida respondents 65 and older wanted senior citizen discounts applied to a wide variety of products and services (Lambert et al. 1980). Another study (reported in *Selling to Seniors* 1989) found that only 13 percent of upscale adults age 55 and older always take advantage of senior discounts. It is not clear why many seniors do not take advantage of special discounts directed exclusively at them. One explanation is that many older adults eligible for these discounts are not aware of them, as the study by Lambert suggested.

With respect to other senior programs, many industry analysts and experts have questioned the effectiveness of senior discounts and senior membership programs. For example, while research studies address the reasons why older adults may not use senior discounts, some point to the widespread availability of these price-saving incentives, which diminishes their effectiveness as a competitive tool (*Maturity Market Perspectives* 1992). Similarly, the effectiveness of senior membership programs has been questioned on the grounds that they may not be cost effective, citing examples of companies that have discontinued them (*Maturity Market Perspectives* 1990).

To summarize, the available research and expert opinions are not clear as to the effectiveness of age-based marketing strategies. The data appear to suggest that such strategies might be most effective when the product/service is not consumed only by the aged, where the opportunity exists for marketers to demonstrate the product's perceived value to the older person by showing that the product is relevant to people in various stages in life.

NEW INSIGHTS

Our research sought to provide answers to this issue by focusing on older adults' responses to age-based marketing strategies in several areas, including senior discounts, age-targeted products, and age-related stimuli in ads. Respondents provided "agree-disagree" answers to statements, and the results are shown in Table 11.1.

A large majority of the 55-and-older respondents were of the opinion that companies should offer discounts based on age. Our older respondents also indicated a relatively strong preference for developing age-segregated sections in print media.

On the subject of age-related stimuli in ads, our research solicited responses to age stereotypes, older spokespersons, and age-targeted products in advertisements. Nearly one in three older adults was found to avoid buying products because their advertisements improperly stereotyped age groups. Only one in ten of the over-55 sample said they pay more attention to ads that show younger people as spokespersons than to those using older people. This finding contradicts that reported by the Gallup Organization (Ward 1989), which showed a substantially higher percentage of older adults liking older models in advertisements. One-third of the older adults in our study disagreed with the statement "There should be less advertising showing older people in situations where they are the authority." Sixteen percent agreed, while the majority expressed no opinion. Finally, 29 percent admitted they like advertisements that show products

Table 11.1
Responses to Age-Based Marketing Strategies

	Strongly/ Somewhat Disagree %	Neither Agree Nor Disagree %	Strongly/ Somewhat Agree %
Senior Discounts			
Companies should offer more discounts to older than to younger adults	17.3	28.9	53.8
Specialized Media Content			
I would prefer magazines or newspapers to have special sections of interest to groups of readers, such as "baby boomers" and "older adults"	17.4	39.8	42.8
Age Stereotypes in Ads			
I have avoided buying products because their advertisements were improperly stereotyping younger or older people	24.9	44.0	31.1
Older Spokespersons in Ads			
I pay more attention to advertisements that show younger people as spokespersons than to those showing older people	46.6	42.0	11.3
There should be less advertising showing older people in situations where they are in authority	33.3	50.6	16.0
Age-Targeted Products in Ads			
I like advertisements that show products especially for older people	21.3	49.6	29.2

Note: Row percentage figures may not add up to 100.0 due to rounding off.

especially for older people, while 21 percent indicated the opposite; the majority expressed no opinion.

Older Consumers Are More Sensitive

Responses to age-based marketing strategies were analyzed and compared among younger (under 55) and older (55+) groups. Table 11.2 shows the results of this analysis.

Older people are more likely than younger adults to approve of com-

Table 11.2
Responses to Age-Based Marketing Strategies among Younger (under 55) and Older (55+) Adults (percentage "strongly/somewhat agree")

	Younger	Older
Senior Discounts		
Companies should offer more discounts to older than to younger adults	43.9	51.7
Specialized Media Content		
I would prefer magazines or newspapers to have special sections of interest to groups of readers, such as "baby boomers" and "older adults"	35.5	42.2
Age Stereotypes in Ads		
I have avoided buying products because their advertisements were improperly stereotyping younger or older people	25.8	31.4
Older Spokespersons in Ads		
I pay more attention to advertisements that show younger people as spokespersons than to those showing older people	14.9	11.4
There should be less advertising showing older people in situations where they are in authority	7.5	15.8
Age-Targeted Products in Ads		
I like advertisements that show products especially for older people	8.6	27.3

panies offering more discounts to older than to younger adults. They are also more likely to prefer magazines with special sections for various age groups and to boycott products or companies whose ads improperly stereotype younger or older adults. This suggests that older adults are more sensitive to age-related marketing stimuli than younger adults.

Older and younger respondents did not show significant differences in levels of attention to younger or older spokespersons. However, older adults were more likely than younger adults to express the opinion that there should be less advertising showing older people in situations where they are in authority. Finally, 27 percent of older people indicated that they liked advertisements that show products especially for older people, compared with only 9 percent of younger adults. This finding contradicts research by Alan Greco and Linda E. Swayne (1992), which found indifference to elderly models featured in display ads for age-neutral products. It might be that the product's suitability to the older person's needs is enhanced by the presence of an older spokesperson. Alternatively, the term *older* may have different connotations in the minds of different age groups.

Sociodemographic Differences

One of our interests in this study was how responses to age-based marketing strategies vary by age in late life. In order to accomplish this objective, responses were categorized by age category (55–64, 65–74, 75+).

Preferences for senior discounts increase slightly with age. Similarly, preferences for special sections in print media increase, but only marginally, with age. Those who have avoided buying products because of their ads are more likely to be found in the 65 to 74 age bracket (34.5%) and are least likely to come from the 75-plus age group (20.4%). While attention to spokespersons of different ages does not change with age, opinions on whether there should be advertisements where older people are in authority show a rather interesting pattern. The group most likely to object to this idea is the 65-to-74 age group, while the 75 and older group is virtually indifferent. Finally, preference for ads that show products especially for older people gradually increases in late life. Again, these findings seem to suggest that the younger age group of mature consumers may try to defend the "younger" age status they were accustomed to before joining the ranks of "seniors," while the older age group may have internalized old-age self-perceptions and feel more comfortable with stimuli that are designed to appeal to them.

Age differences in responses vary according to the older person's background characteristics. For example, preference for ads showing older spokespersons increases with age only among those with low education, while only the most educated respond favorably with increasing age to senior discounts. To determine the "pure" effects of age, the relationship between age and responses to the same age-based marketing stimuli was analyzed by removing the effects of other confounding factors. The results were fairly consistent with those obtained by analyzing differences in responses by each specific age group, with the exception of opinions on the presence or absence of older people as the authority in ads, where the relationship was a curvilinear one. Instead, the relationship found in that analysis suggested a positive orientation among the "young-olds" (55–64) and the "old-olds" (75+). These findings suggest that the younger group (55–64) may not perceive these stimuli to apply to them personally, while those in the oldest group have internalized old age and do not try to defend a younger self-concept.

Few gender differences emerged in responses to age-targeted marketing strategies. It was found that female older adults are more likely than their male counterparts to prefer special content in print media of interest to groups of readers including older adults (44.2% versus 39.0%). Similarly, older females are more likely than males to prefer advertisements that show products especially for older people (31.4% versus 25.4%). These findings suggest that age-based marketing strategies aimed at older people may be more effective among older women than among older men.

When responses were analyzed by geographic region (east, north, south, and west), a wide variation in many orientations toward age-based marketing strategies became evident. The analysis revealed that mature adults living in western states are more likely than those living in northern states (58.8% versus 48.5%) to approve of more discounts being offered to older than to younger adults. A larger percentage (45.1%) of easterners than southerners (38.6%) would like to see specialized content in print media targeted at specific age groups. The same geographic groups also reported different propensities to boycott products due to improper age stereotyping in advertisements (33.7% versus 28.4%). Mature adults living in northern states are more likely than those living in western states (19.2% versus 13.0%) to prefer less advertising showing older people in situations where they are in authority. A larger percentage of easterners (31.2%) are likely to indicate preference for advertisements that show products especially for older people, in comparison to mature people living in the south who show the lowest preference for such advertisements (24.4%). Thus, these findings suggest that age-targeted strategies are relatively more effective for older consumers who live in eastern than southern states.

Variations in responses to age-targeted marketing strategies by level of income were also uncovered in our study. When agreement responses were classified by level of household income of the respondents (under $30,000, $30,000-$49,999; and $50,000 or more), several differences emerged. Overall, there was a tendency to give less favorable responses to age-targeted marketing strategies with increasing income. Let's consider senior discounts: while 56.8 percent of those in households with less than $30,000 in annual income agreed that there should be more discounts available to older than to younger adults, the percentage among those with incomes in excess of $50,000 dropped to 46.2 percent. Similarly, preference for specialized content in print media targeted at different age groups declines with income, with 44.2 percent and 32.2 of the older adults in the lowest and highest income groups, respectively, reporting such preferences. Upper-income mature adults not only show less favorable orientations toward age-based strategies, but they are also less likely to respond to such stimuli. For example, while more than 30 percent of the lower- and middle-income groups indicated that they had avoided buying products due to improper age stereotyping in ads, the percentage drops to 22.7 percent among those with high incomes, suggesting a lower sensitivity to age stereotyping in ads. A similar decline with higher income emerged with respect to preferences for advertisements that show products especially for older people. Thus, the age-targeted marketing stimuli appear to be most effective among lower-income older adults.

Responses by Need-Based Clusters

The four psychographic clusters based on needs were also analyzed with respect to their reactions to age-targeted marketing stimuli. Some interesting variations emerged across these clusters.

The dependent frail group is most likely to prefer discounts targeted at seniors rather than younger adults, with 55.7 percent of them expressing such preferences. This compares with 45.5 percent agreement by struggling full-nesters, the lowest of all four groups. The dependent frail are also more likely to prefer specialized print media content of interest to various age groups, in comparison to young insecureds who express the lowest preference (44.8% versus 35.1%). Young insecureds, on the other hand, are the group least likely to report avoiding the purchase of products due to improper age stereotyping, with about one in four of them (24.3%) reporting such behavior. This compares to 31.9 percent among self-sufficients, the group expressing the highest propensity to engage in such a behavior.

The propensity to report lower preference for older spokespersons portrayed in authority in ads is the highest among the dependent frail (20.9%) and lowest among struggling full-nesters (11.4%). One-third of the dependent frail (34.0%), approximately 10 percent more than any other group, indicated preference for advertisements that show products especially for older people. Thus, responses to age-based marketing strategy differ on the basis of the older person's needs.

Responses by Gerontographic Groups

Finally, responses to age-based marketing strategies were analyzed by gerontographic cluster. The variations in responses across individuals classified into the four clusters were much wider than those obtained by other factors. Table 11.3 shows the results of this analysis.

Ailing outgoers are particularly receptive to senior discounts, with nearly two-thirds of them expressing a positive opinion on companies that offer such money-saving incentives. This figure compares to 40 percent of healthy hermits, the group least likely to favor these incentives. The same two groups gave extreme responses to the idea of having special sections in print media targeted at various age groups.

With respect to older adults' responses to advertisements, healthy hermits are least likely to report product boycott due to improper age stereotyping in ads, and healthy indulgers are most likely to be offended by such ads and to respond as a result. There appears to be a slight inclination

Table 11.3
Responses to Age-Based Marketing Strategies by Gerontographic Clusters (percentage "strongly/somewhat agree")

	Healthy Hermits	Ailing Outgoers	Frail Recluses	Healthy Indulgers
Senior Discounts				
Companies should offer more discounts to older than to younger adults	40.27	65.92	61.49	50.39
Specialized Media Content				
I would prefer magazines or newspapers to have special sections of interest to groups of readers, such as "baby boomers" and "older adults"	31.78	53.70	39.19	34.65
Age Stereotypes in Ads				
I have avoided buying products because their advertisements were improperly stereotyping younger or older people	27.12	31.51	29.05	33.07
Older Spokespersons in Ads				
I pay more attention to advertisements that show younger people as spokespersons than to those showing older people	46.30	40.19	45.95	40.94
There should be less advertising showing older people where they are in authority	33.15	32.15	27.70	30.71
Age-Targeted Products in Ads				
I like advertisements that show products especially for older people	17.81	36.66	25.68	26.77

among the healthy hermits and frail recluses to pay more attention to ads that show younger people as spokespersons than to those showing older people, while a larger percentage of healthy hermits (33.1%) than frail recluses (27.7%) prefers less advertising showing older people in situations in which they are the authority. Finally, ailing outgoers are twice as likely as healthy hermits to express affective orientations toward ads that show products especially for older people. Collectively, these findings highlight the value of gerontographic characteristics of the mature market in assessing the likelihood of the segment's responses to age-targeted strategies.

SUMMARY AND IMPLICATIONS

The research presented in this chapter suggests that older Americans do not respond to age-based marketing strategies in a uniform manner.

Their responses appear to vary according to the type of strategy or offering (such as senior discounts or use of older models in ads) and specific characteristics of the older person. Background characteristics that determine inclination to respond to age-targeted marketing stimuli include demographics, lifestyles, and gerontographics. The problem of assessing the effects of age-based commercial stimuli is further aggravated by differences in the older person's perceptions of such stimuli, since many may respond positively but might think that the question or statement does not apply to them personally (Moschis 1992b). Many older people not only do not identify with other older people, but also their definition of an "older person" varies according to demographic and psychological factors. For example, the older the person, the higher the age that defines "old age," since most people do not consider themselves to be old at any age.

These findings suggest that a great deal of caution must be exercised when developing and offering products and services that are not age-neutral. Given that different mature consumers may respond differently, marketers need to consider those segments that are likely to respond most favorably to such offerings. Segmentation by gerontographic characteristics appears to be an effective way of developing strategies for different target groups. Marketers should also keep in mind that heterogeneity in responses means that age-based strategies might offend older Americans who do not respond to age-based incentives. Thus, the safest strategy appears to be that which maximizes responses from those who respond favorably and minimizes adverse reactions from those segments of older Americans who tend to respond unfavorably to age-targeted marketing stimuli.

PART V

SUMMARY AND RECOMMENDATIONS

12

Guidelines for Developing Marketing Strategies

This book presents new evidence that helps increase our understanding of the aging population and how to market to them. The information presented comes from several studies. Some of the information reinforces existing beliefs, while other data help us gain new insights and provide the bases for developing effective marketing strategies.

Although both gerontologists and marketers acknowledge that age is not a good predictor of behavior, common practices in defining older segments of the population still focus on age. Using age to define the mature segment has been traditionally an easy approach, since government agencies compile data on wealth and other indicaters of size and composition of this segment. However, age-based definitions lose much of their appeal when one moves into the marketing arena. This is because marketers estimate demand for products and services on the basis of interest, ability to buy, and access to a particular market offer, in addition to using demographic bases such as age. Of course, there is a higher likelihood that a need for a product or service exists in a given age segment, but the selection of an age cutoff point such as 50 or 55 is completely arbitrary. For example, while about half of the 65-plus population has arthritis, targeting this segment would ignore half of the market. Similarly, targeting the 30 million people aged 50 to 65 for travel and leisure services (because they have the highest income) could leave out a large segment of the 32 million people age 65 and over who may not have as much income but have more time to travel. Furthermore, age-based statistics that report demand for products on a household basis are confounded with household size and tend to show decreasing demand with age that often reflects reduced household size. On the other hand, statistics based on responses given by a single person in the household may not accurately reflect the age and consumer behavior of other family members.

MARKET SEGMENTATION AND TARGETING

In segmenting the mature market, the focus should be more on the person's *stage in life* rather than on one's age. Life stages can be defined in terms of social, psychological, and health-related circumstances that people face. Much of the research in social sciences shows that people age not just biologically or physically, but also socially and even spiritually; they age differently and at different rates. It is often the composite of changes in these aging processes that affects behavior. Quite often it is social demands or expectations that affect one's aging, as in the case of retirement and becoming a grandparent, or it could be a chronic condition (e.g., arthritis) that can slow us down and make us feel the need for certain products. Such events can occur at different points in life, or they may never occur for some people, causing them to experience fewer subsequent needs for certain products and services.

Today, it is possible for those who seek to define the mature market in terms of life stages to obtain the necessary information that defines people's physiological, psychological, and social aging. Information is available on variables such as health status (medical history), interests and lifestyles (e.g., publications read), and family life-cycle stage (e.g., retirement, empty nest). When these types of variables are used simultaneously, they are likely to produce life stages that can predict consumer behavior better than age per se. Specifically, the four life stages suggested by the gerontographics model (see Chapter 4, specifically Figure 4.1) appear to have much appeal over traditional segmentation models based on age and lifestyles. This model could be used in concert with other data for maximum effectiveness.

Target Marketing

Information presented in this book suggests that the mature market is heterogeneous. *Market heterogeneity* suggests that using one strategy for the entire market is not likely to be effective. Companies marketing to the mature population have the choice of going after select segments of this market or trying to appeal to all subsegments. This decision can often be made by considering factors such as company resources and objectives. For example, smaller companies usually cannot afford the cost of designing different strategies to appeal to many subsegments. Instead, they go after select segments and try to develop market "niches." Should one decide to use differentiated marketing—that is, different strategies for different segments—a number of guidelines should be followed.

First, companies should address the issue of *profitability* in developing different arrays of products and services to appeal to different subsegments. The question is, are differences in needs or preferences in the various subsegments significant enough to justify the development of differentiated marketing? The smaller the differences, the fewer the potential sales lost due to undifferentiated marketing; the greater the differences, the larger the losses. Conversely, the greater the differences, the higher the costs of developing marketing programs to meet different needs and, therefore, the incremental revenues needed to cover these costs.

Second, one should examine the *impact of marketing strategies on other segments* the organization attempts to reach. Unfortunately, this is often a serious omission. Firms that try to reach older consumers should not alienate younger consumers in the process, since the latter group may end up being more profitable in the long run, if they are retained as customers.

In developing marketing strategy, companies should try to *use sound bases* for decision making. There are diverse opinions on how to market to older consumers. This is due in part to the fact that marketing is not a science. Strategies must constantly change to fit changing conditions in the business environment. However, when marketing to older Americans, one should use the available knowledge about the older population that has accumulated over several decades in various areas of social sciences. There is presently a wide gap between what marketers do and what knowledge from various fields suggests they should do. For example, take psychographic or lifestyle models, which are based on personality theories. The results of several decades of research by Bernice Neugarten (1977), a noted gerontologist, show that personality changes little after age 30, while extensive reviews of studies on personality and consumer behavior over several decades by University of California at Los Angeles (UCLA) professor Harold Kassarjian show that personality is a relatively weak predictor of consumer behavior ("Personality and Consumer Behavior" 1991). Similarly, empirical tests of VALS (Values and Life Styles) show that psychographics can only explain consumer behavior 2 to 3 percent of the time, leaving 97 percent of reasons unexplained; and they may not be as good predictors as demographics (Novak and McEvoy 1990). Yet, psychographic and personality models have been heavily used as bases for marketing to older people.

Finally, try to *understand older customers*. The reasons older consumers behave the way they do are several, and no single theory or approach is likely to provide adequate explanations. Behavior is influenced by a host of factors, and recent efforts in several disciplines of social sciences aimed at understanding human behavior have been focusing on incorporating several factors stemming from different research traditions. To assume there is a single explanation or view of why older people behave in a certain fashion is likely to increase the chances for marketing mistakes. For example, using solely psychological or psychographic models as bases for decision making would be extremely risky, since they provide inadequate explanations for consumer behavior in late life. Furthermore, because the mature market is heterogeneous, some older consumers are more likely to behave according to a given model. For example, frail recluses may behave more according to a physiological model, with their consumer behaviors greatly influenced by physical requirements and frailties. On the other hand, healthy hermits may behave more in line with the psychological model, since physical limitations do not greatly affect their behavior. This suggests the need to understand the reasons selected targets behave the way they do, and the models most applicable to a given segment.

Undifferentiated Marketing

Developing segment-based strategies for targeting the mature market and specific subsegments may not always be advantageous or feasible. A company may not be able to commit resources for differentiated marketing, the costs may not justify the incremental benefits, or the strategies aimed at the mature market or its subsegments may adversely affect younger customers. Under such circumstances an undifferentiated strategy should be considered. How can one design an effective "universal" strategy? Segmentation is still a viable strategic tool. However, the purpose here is to find out the needs and attitudes that are both *common and different* among younger and older people or among subsegments of the mature market. In doing so, the strategy can be developed on the basis of similarities, avoiding products and communications that are likely to get different responses from the marketplace. For example, both younger and older consumers would like to see easier-to-open packages, according to results of many surveys, and company efforts along this line would constitute an effective marketing tactic. The focus should be on emphasizing commonalities and deemphasizing differences in attitudes and preferences of the market.

PRODUCT POSITIONING

There are several competitive tactics a company should consider using in order to appeal to older consumers. A company can achieve the greatest competitive advantage by offering something older consumers presently need but are not getting. This is commonly known as *positioning strategy*. While there are variations across subsegments and industries, there are four common themes that emerge from studies of older consumers that companies should use to position themselves and achieve a nonprice-competitive advantage: risk reduction, functionality, convenience, and familiarity or simplicity (Moschis 1992b).

Risk Reduction

Every purchase involves risk taking, since buyers cannot accurately foresee the consequence of their choice. Buyers may reduce risk by using information "cues" that are accurate predictors of purchase outcome and expected level of satisfaction. Older buyers are more likely than younger buyers to try to reduce risk by using cues such as brand names, product or service warranties, and liberal return policies. Older people are inclined to use several other risk-reduction strategies such as patronizing only reputable stores, "buying American," and buying high-priced or quality products. Marketers should stress the appropriate product or service attributes that help older consumers reduce risk, depending on the type of product or service they sell. For example, a well-established firm may emphasize its name and long-term existence to convey the image of dependability, while a relatively new firm should communicate warranties, after-sale service, and other offerings that create a low-risk image of buying their product or service.

Functionality

Product functionality is another dimension along which companies can successfully position themselves. In comparison with younger buyers, mature consumers are more concerned with what the product does for them to address their day-to-day needs, and not so much with how the product looks or what others think of them because of their product preferences. Attributes such as "easy to use" or operate, comfort, efficiency, and practicality are highly valued by older buyers. Older Americans are not as impressed with "peripheral" or "excess" product or service attributes as are younger consumers. Companies are likely to be more successful if they sell the core product or service separately from auxiliary features. For example, automobiles could be better sold to older Americans by selling the various options or "add-ons" separately from the basic product, rather than trying to sell automobiles loaded with options and features. Functionality also means designing or redesigning products and features so that they are easy to manipulate and generally meet the physiological deficiencies associated with aging. This suggests that positioning on functionality would have a great appeal among frail recluses.

Convenience

The term *convenience* has different meanings to people at different stages in life. Time saving is a convenience factor of greater importance to younger people and to some older people (especially to healthy indulgers), while ease of purchasing and using a product and service are of greater importance to older consumers (especially to frail recluses). Examples of convenience features in the latter category include a store's access to public transportation, ease of reading product information on packages, ease of locating and removing items from shelves, easy-to-open products and packages, and ease of paying for products and services. Marketers and retailers have much to gain by offering services along these lines.

Familiarity/Simplicity

Mature consumers are more likely to accept a new product, remember a message, or shop at a place when they can relate the present situation to what they already know. With age, the human brain loses its ability to evaluate new and unfamiliar stimuli, and older people find it increasingly difficult to use new information from their commercial environments. Therefore, new information, whether in the form of a message or a new product, becomes easier for older people to use when it "fits" into existing knowledge. This means that, for example, new products should use "family" names (the familiar name of the company that makes them), and new information in the media should be related to what the older market already knows.

While these are not the only factors that motivate the consumer behavior of older people, companies that develop strategies focusing on these factors are likely to benefit a great deal.

DEVELOPING MARKETING PROGRAMS

Companies may use a number of strategies to compete with others for the mature market share. Usually, strategies are in the form of either price or nonprice competition. The first includes offering products and services at reduced prices or special sales, coupons, "deals," and the like. Nonprice competition, on the other hand, involves the delivery of nonmonetary benefits such as unique product features, promotional appeals, and a variety of services. Nonprice offerings have special "value added" nonmonetary benefits older adults are likely to find attractive such as convenience, after-sale service, and information useful in decision making.

Pricing Decisions

Companies marketing to older consumers should avoid placing great emphasis on price or monetary appeals; instead, they should try to compete on nonprice bases. There are several reasons for this. First, price offerings can be matched quickly and in identical fashion by other companies. Furthermore, the findings presented in this book suggest that money-saving incentives such as coupons are not likely to induce brand switching but only purchase of the brand the older person usually buys. On the other hand, a firm can create a differential advantage such as a new product design, develop an advertising appeal, or train its personnel to be sensitive to the needs of older customers, all of which would be much more difficult for competition to match. Second, as more competitors begin to offer various forms of price reduction, the competitive effects of these strategies are quickly diminished, cutting into industry profits. A good example of an industry where senior discounts have lost their impact is the airline industry where, according to a survey by the Mature Market Group, seventeen of the eighteen airlines studied offer senior discounts (*Maturity Market Perspectives* 1992). Discontinuing these offerings could affect customer retention rates, since there is evidence to suggest that older people are particularly sensitive to being denied offerings they have been accustomed to receiving at a low cost or fee (Noeske 1987). In light of potential customer losses to competitors who continue to provide these offerings, firms should provide a different package of benefits to keep their competitive edge.

New Products

The information presented in this book suggests that new products should be developed and positioned in line with the needs of older consumers. Not only should these be developed to satisfy specific needs such as independence, security, and sociability, but the various product benefits should also be made obvious to the older person. This is particularly imperative for new technology-based products and services, where the benefits should provide strong incentives for the older person to overcome fears and apprehensions about such products. Marketers must take into consideration the older person's declining ability to process information and reluctance to use new products, and they should try to develop products that are easy to understand and use. Thus, the success of an innovation aimed at older people appears to depend on two major factors: (1) benefits that address key needs of older people and can be easily communicated to them; and (2) the marketer's ability to make the product simple to use. One strategy to accomplish the second point is to make new products whose operation is similar to that of an existing product with which the older person is already familiar.

Another strategy is to appeal to the older person's younger relatives who might feel more comfortable with the new product, helping their aged relative see its potential benefits. One of the most interesting findings reported in this book is that many of the products expected to appeal to older adults are of equal or greater appeal to younger adults. This finding suggests that many younger people who are likely to be caregivers might want these products for their old relatives. However, it would appear to be dangerous to market new products exclusively to older consumers since this might not only keep potential younger buyers away but could also alienate the mature market. Finally, branding strategies that use family names (i.e., existing names for other products) are likely to be favorably received by older Americans.

Distribution

Shopping may have a different meaning for older than for younger consumers. For example, shopping may provide opportunities for socializing, or it may be a leisure experience; it could also be a form of exercise and could fill idle time. Marketers and retailers should not simply assume that older people go to a store only to buy products but rather should position retail outlets as vehicles that enable the older person to satisfy a variety of other needs. Whatever the reasons for shopping, the retail environment should be easily accessible, simple, pleasant, and safe.

In late life, personal services are valued more by older shoppers who may have difficulty locating merchandise, reading product information, and making a decision. Similarly, the older person's inclination to prefer one-stop shopping with increasing age suggests the value of a strategy that involves placing several diverse product lines under the same roof. Thus, retailers are encouraged to place several departments in their stores (e.g., bank and pharmacy) and offer nontraditional services the older person might need such as photocopying machines and film development services. Obtaining services, which is perceived to be a chore, from the same place increases the value of the retail outlet because it minimizes the older person's effort and risk in obtaining them. Safety is an important concern among older persons. Because of the older person's concern with safety, one might be willing to, for example, obtain cash from a bank located inside a supermarket rather than go to an automatic teller machine (ATM) at an isolated location.

Finally, the development of distribution strategies should take into account the diversity of the mature market. For example, clustering of stores older people are likely to patronize might be more important to frail recluses than to healthy indulgers. Various forms of direct marketing should also be considered in the development of a company's distribution strategy.

Promotion

Promotional strategies for the mature market can be classified into two categories: those that focus on age-irrelevant decisions and those that focus on age-targeted stimuli. With respect to the first type of promotional decisions, the research presented here suggests that the company's promotional mix should vary depending upon the characteristics of the market segment, the nature of the product or service, and the objectives of the communicator. For example, healthy indulgers are responsive to in-store promotions, while frail recluses are responsive to mass media advertisements. Second, the type of the product dictates the type of promotional mix that should be used. As the findings of research studies presented here suggest, although mass media have become important sources of consumer information with age, personal sources are used whenever available, especially in the case of important decisions. One must keep in mind that older consumers need assistance in buying products and services, and salespeople are often an important source of consumer information. Older people may hesitate, however, to approach salespeople because they may not want to admit their dependency, or they may be concerned with the salesperson's unwillingness or inability to be of assistance. As the results of our study showed, older people do not consult salespeople often, but a lot of them would like to have a personal adviser whom they can trust at the store they patronize. Thus, training salespeople to be more understanding and sensitive of the older person's needs should produce results.

With respect to age-based promotional strategies, the research cited here suggests a great deal of caution in developing promotional stimuli based on age. Some older Americans tend to respond favorably while others tend to react negatively to promotions directed at older people. Thus, the task at hand appears to be a careful segmentation of the mature market, developing age-based strategies that could appeal to some segments but would not have adverse effects on other segments that also contain prospective customers. It is safer to develop intergenerational appeals and stress product benefits that might appeal to older adults rather than risk creating age-targeted promotions, which might not only position a product or service as one for older people but also risk alienating the older market.

EVALUATING STRATEGIES

The area of evaluation is one of the most difficult and challenging aspects of any complete marketing program. How can marketers tell if their strategies and tactics aimed at the older population work? At the outset, let's remind ourselves of the high product failure rates—in the range of two in three—that companies experience when marketing to consumers in general. These ratios occur even though our knowledge about market behavior is greater than specific knowledge about older consumers. Therefore, marketing mistakes are likely to be common not only due to limited knowledge about this segment, but also due to the fact that failure rates are high across all types of consumers.

Marketing strategies and tactics can be evaluated from three different perspectives: the company's, the consumer's, and an outside observer's (such as a researcher's or a consultant's). A company may evaluate the success of a strategy by looking at criteria such as increase in sales or enrollment into a program. The drawback of this method is that the company never knows whether response is due to the company's strategies, due to competitors' strategies, or from the specific market. For example, the Wendy's commercial "where is the beef" involving an older woman, Clara Peller, was considered very effective by management and advertising executives, but an increase in sales could have come from those who found it most appealing—young people. Similarly, the strategy's effectiveness may be neutralized in the light of heavy competitive response or equally effective strategies such as senior discount programs.

Asking consumers to evaluate the effectiveness of a strategy also has drawbacks since older persons may not be able to verbalize their opinion or they may try to give "rational" explanations in part because they may not be aware of how the company's offerings have affected their behavior. Finally, an outside observer may try to assess the firm's strategies by comparing them to some norm—existing knowledge, consumer preferences, or other accepted practices in the industry. The problem with this method is that there are diverse views on what constitutes effective marketing to the mature market, and knowledge often differs from practice.

A 1992 study of approximately 500 companies conducted by the author at the Center for Mature Consumer Studies found a lack of consensus as to what constitutes an effective strategy among decision makers in various industries; and there was disagreement even among those in specific industries. There were companies that had implemented strategies even though decision makers did not think they were effective, perhaps in order to keep up with competition. There were tactical strategies that were not considered to be important by the majority. For example, use of credit is not considered to be important by most decision makers in every industry reported, when the results of studies reported in this book as well as other research (Mathur and Moschis 1992) suggest that this may not be the case. Given the differences in knowledge as to what constitutes an effective strategy, how should a firm go about evaluating the effectiveness of its strategies? Four guidelines are recommended: establishing criteria, developing industry-specific evaluation strategies, focusing on consumer preferences, and monitoring changes.

Establish Criteria

Marketing strategies should be evaluated in the context of the firm's overall marketing program. A successful strategy is not the one that merely increases sales or enrollments into membership programs, but the one with maximum impact on overall company goals over a specific period of time. Thus, one must address issues of cost-effectiveness and the impact of these strategies on other parts of the business operations and the company as a whole. For example, consider membership programs implemented by hospitals, banks, and the travel industry. They may not be cost-effective because the same resources spent on other marketing activities (e.g., staff training) may result in higher retention of present customers and greater profitability. However, they could be considered successful to the extent that a large percentage of members can be cross-sold other (additional) services or products. On the other hand, what appears to be successful may not be cost- effective, and therefore may not be successful. For example, coupons tend to induce older shoppers to buy the same products they usually buy, resulting in minimal brand switching. Similarly, "senior days" specials may simply motivate those who already patronize the same store to shop at different times rather than getting them to switch stores. Such programs may not generate enough incremental sales and might not result in significant reduction in operating costs to be considered successful.

Industry-Specific Evaluation

Evaluation of marketing programs and strategies should be industry-specific—that is, what may be effective marketing strategies for some products or services may not be effective for other products. This is because the marketplace in general does not behave in a homogeneous manner; consumers show different patterns of behavior according to the product or service they buy. For example, free samples are more effective in introducing packaged goods and are less relevant in the marketing of services.

Focus on Consumer Preferences

Marketing and programs should be evaluated in line with consumer perceptions for two reasons. First, what marketers know or practice may be based on inaccurate or outdated information since the marketplace constantly changes. Second, because of great heterogeneity of the mature market, the effectiveness of a given marketing strategy or tactic may depend on the type of market targeted. Companies that evaluate the effectiveness of their programs from the customer's perspective are likely to reduce biases or erroneous interpretations of the value of such programs.

Perhaps the key direct indicators of successful marketing strategies are measures of consumer satisfaction with the firm's offerings. An effective way to accomplish this is to measure satisfaction before implementing a particular strategy or tactics, and then again later after consumers have had the opportunity to learn about the firm's offerings and respond.

Monitor Changes

The marketplace constantly changes and so do business strategies. The changing environment creates opportunities for companies to develop and market new products and services in order to survive and prosper. Companies that are proactive rather than reactive to these changes stand a better chance to stay competitive. In order to do this, marketers should constantly monitor trends in the environment, and although the future cannot be predicted with a great accuracy, trends can suggest ways helpful in designing long-term strategy. Companies interested in planning ahead to position themselves effectively in the mature market should focus on three major changes.

New Opportunities

Organizations marketing to older Americans should be constantly looking for opportunities to more effectively serve the older population. Opportunities are likely to arise from the external and internal business environment. Technological innovations and changes in legislation are examples of changes in the environment external to a firm that can create opportunities for companies to capitalize upon. For example, improvement in technologies could create opportunities for delivering products and services in a cost-effective manner as in the case of home health-monitoring systems. The second set of opportunities, internal to a company, arises out of the firm's capabilities to better serve the mature population in relation to the capabilities of its competitors. Over time, a company's differential advantage may be diminished as more competitors use similar strategies, as in the case of senior discounts. Meanwhile, shifts in consumer preferences may create opportunities for a company to reposition itself to better serve customer needs.

Tomorrow's Market

Marketers need to be continuously developing and testing strategies on a constantly changing mature population. What works today may not work tomorrow because future cohorts' responses to marketing offerings might be heavily influenced by different circumstances. For example, it has been estimated that by the time today's baby boomers reach age 65, they will have spent an average of eleven years of their lives in front of television, considerably less than today's elderly. Marketing planners should keep in mind the lifestyles of tomorrow's mature Americans and the environment they are likely to live in. For example, all the evidence seems to point to tougher times ahead for baby boomers. These individuals are likely to be living in smaller size households due to increasing life expectancy, higher divorce rates, and fewer children to care for them, resulting in higher cost per capita for maintaining these households. As a result, they will be more likely to need long-term care services than today's elderly population. In addition, the rising cost of long-term care and the baby boomers' lower propensity to save (patterns of personality change little after midlife) are likely to create enormous problems for tomorrow's older population, posing challenges to policymakers and opportunities for marketers to develop products similar to reverse mortgage plans to solve the future financial problems of today's baby boomers.

A Changing Environment

One final change businesses will have to monitor is how the mature market changes its environment. The traditional view of how the market responds to business practices is a passive one. That is, consumers are viewed as passive actors either accepting or rejecting products and services companies develop to satisfy their needs. Future cohorts with great political, economic, and social power are likely to play a more profound role in dictating company policy. Organized groups represented by organizations such as the American Association of Retired Persons (AARP) are likely to exert a greater influence on company strategic decisions and public policy issues. The area of health care is on the list of priorities. Businesses are likely to be faced with greater constraints with respect to the way they advertise, how they present information on packages and labels, and the types of product lines they develop. Efforts by companies such as the Whirlpool Corporation to develop appliances for the handicapped, which is a rather unprofitable product line, are early signs that businesses are likely to increasingly experience public pressure in the not too distant future. Thus, the concept of "social responsibility" would have to be modified to embrace many needs of the aged.

Appendixes

Appendix A
Sample of List of Needs and Need Satisfiers

Needs of Mature Consumers	Technologies Capable of Satisfying Needs	Existing or Emerging Products/Services Capable of Satisfying Needs	Additional Suggested Products/Services for Satisfying Needs
1. **Physiological needs**, due to decrease in ability to:			
a. hear (higher frequency sounds)	Technologies that modify/apply enhancement of total communications, reduce background noise, and offer alternatives to sound-dependent communication	.hearing aids	(Example) . phone devices to aid the hearing impaired-i.e., amplifiers _____ _____ _____ _____ _____ _____ _____
b. see (decreased focusing speed, sensitivity to light, distortion of colors, visual efficiency, and reduction of total field of vision)	Technologies or products that help: 1) deliver information at controlled speeds; 2) size and spacing of lettering; 3) offer adjustable lighting; 4) settings, signs, colors and instrumentation panels on appliances	.teletext .optical character recognition .voice activated products	(Example) . phone devices (add on) to aid the sight impaired _____ _____ _____ _____ _____ _____

Appendix B

Sample of Hypotheses (implications for marketing) Based on Theory and Research Findings

Findings and Theories	Hypotheses (Implications) Based on Findings/Theories
The information-processing abilities of the aging person undergo significant changes. With increasing age, older persons process information less efficiently because: (a) they are becoming unable to see and use concrete information (b) they are becoming increasingly unable to differentiate between stimuli (c) they experience short-term memory loss	Biophysical changes common in later stages in the person's life affect his/her consumer behavior in the marketplace. With increasing age, the older consumer is: (a) less likely to use product information (b) more likely to need personal in-store assistance in locating and evaluating products (c) less likely to recall and use information in advertisements
With increasing age, the older person makes greater use of the mass media to compensate for other kinds of loss, including social contact; s/he uses the mass media more for information than entertainment purposes	Older adults are more likely to: (a) prefer informational over emotional advertising messages (b) prefer special "news" programs for older adults (e.g., health, money management, leisure) over regular programming (c) prefer special sections for elderly in newspapers (e.g., "For Mature Reader") over existing format (d) prefer specialized magazines for older adults (e.g., Modern Maturity) than magazines for younger adults
The older consumer prefers using cash for products/services purchased; s/he makes little use of credit cards	Mature consumers will be more likely than their younger counterparts to prefer: (a) cash discounts (b) extended non-interest payment plans (c) a larger number of "cash only" registers (d) methods which make check cashing easier (e.g., check approval cards)
Older persons perceive higher risk associated with the purchase of new products than younger consumers	Older adults are more likely than their younger counterparts to try new products when: (a) they are given free samples (b) they can buy the product on a "free-trial" basis (c) they can initially purchase the product in small quantities/ packages (d) they can buy them at reputable stores

Findings/Theories	Hypotheses (Implications) Based on Findings/Theories
Mature consumers are portrayed as ineffective and passive in the mass media; they have been under-represented and poorly stereotyped.	Older consumers will be more likely than their younger counterparts to: (a) favorably respond to advertising messages that depict older consumers in situations where they are the authority (b) prefer advertisements that use older spokespersons well-known for their abilities and vitality (c) prefer advertisements that show products especially for older people (d) prefer stores employing older people
The older person's desire to maintain economic independence increases with age; it is reflected in greater preoccupation with "money-saving" offerings	Older adults are more likely than younger adults to: (a) prefer stores that offer discounts to mature consumers (b) prefer shopping at stores during special "economy shopping days" (c) buy products "on sale" (d) save and use coupons
Shopping is a major social activity for older persons, in spite of physical limitations or inconvenience	In relation to younger adults, older individuals are more likely to prefer: (a) valet parking (b) shopping at a store location in multi-store areas (e.g., malls) (c) public transportation to and from shopping areas (d) organized social activities (e.g., "lunch and shop" days, senior citizen product demonstration days)
Older shoppers welcome special treatment	Older shoppers are more likely than younger shoppers to prefer retail outlets that: (a) assign older adults to a "special customers" service person to call for assistance (b) have in-store special service centers for older shoppers (c) offer special product demonstrations of interest to older adults (e.g., fashion shows) (d) provide home-delivery and in-house services

Appendix C
Orientations Toward Various Types of Marketing Practices and Stimuli

Marketing Area	Sample Items (5-point Agree-Disagree Scales)	Marketing Area	Sample Items (5-point Agree-Disagree Scales)
Advertising	I have bought products/service because I like their ads	Packages/labels	I often find letters on packages and labels too small to read
Brands	I prefer a certain brand of most products I buy	Stores	I prefer doing most of my shopping in the same stores I have always shopped in
New products	I like to try something new every time I am in the store	Direct marketing (At-home shopping)	I often order items from catalogs and magazines
Coupons/discounts	I use coupons with my purchase whenever I can	In-store displays	I am attracted to special displays in a store
Salespeople	When I go shopping, I often ask salespeople to help me buy things for myself	"Sales"	A special sale will tempt me to buy an item I hadn't planned on buying
Store location	I don't mind paying high prices if the store is conveniently located	Technology-based products/services	Older people should learn to use electronic gadgets and services that make life easier
Store layout	Most stores do not have enough "cash only" registers	Prices	Stores should charge less when a person pays "cash" for products or services
After-sale-service	I would like to have a personal advisor at places where I buy products and services whom I could call for assistance and complaints	Product-return policy	I would not buy a new product unless I knew it would be easy to return it
		Free samples	I would hesitate buying a new health care item if I have not used a free sample of it
Method of payment	I like to pay cash for most things I buy	Warrantees/ guarantees	I pay little attention to product warrantees and guarantees
Product use	I often find packages and containers difficult to open	(Dis)satisfaction/ complaining	I make it a point to let others know of products and services I am not happy with

Appendix D
Examples of Products/Services Capable of Satisfying Select Needs of Older Adults

Needs	Product/Service Descriptions	Measures
Physiological (e.g., due to short-term memory loss)	"An electronic calendar in your watch or telephone that would remind you to do certain things." (S)	
Companionship/interpersonal (as a result of social isolation, immobility and loss of face-to-face interaction)	"A telephone number that would connect you with a small number of people wishing to have conversation on a variety of topics on given dates and times." (S)	For each product/service, level of desirability is measured using 2 scales:
Information (due to increasing importance of certain issues)	"Ability to request certain TV programs to be aired at any time you wanted to watch them." (S)	(a) Probability of usage (measure on a 5-point "Definitely would use" to "Definitely would not")
Domestic assistance (due to physical impairment, isolation, and need for convenience)	"Ability to pay all utility bills in one bill, with the total amount automatically subtracted from your bank account or charged to your bank card." (C)	(b) Maximum price respondent would be willing to pay for the product or service (e.g., per month, per call
	"Special assistance phone numbers, with the operator helping in locating the nearest certified person available to provide a service (like repairs)." (C)	
Stay-active (e.g., postponing retirement or reentering the labor market)	"A club providing services such as volunteer programs, a placement bureau for retirees, courses, and social activities such as fashion shows for all ages." (S)	
Survival and security/protection	"An alarm system that would monitor your personal health, diagnose undesirable conditions and alert you or automatically notify an emergency unit." (C)	
	"An alarm system that would monitor your home, check undesirable conditions and notify the appropriate person or emergency unit." (C)	

Note: (S) denotes "simple" product/service; (C) denotes "complex" product/service

Appendix E
Demographic Characteristics of 55+ Sample (weighted responses)

Age	Number	Percent
55-64	432	44.1
65-74	315	32.2
75+	232	23.7
	979	100.0

Sex		
Male	423	44.4
Female	529	55.6
	952	100.0

Education		
High school or less	359	37.2
Some college	323	33.3
College graduate	285	29.5
	967	100.0

Marital Status		
Married	735	75.3
Widowed/Divorced/Separated/ Never Married	241	24.7
	976	100.0

Race		
Black	17	1.8
White	923	96.4
Other	17	1.8
	957	100.0

Income		
Under 10,000	77	8.2
10,000-19,999	206	22.1
20,000-29,999	214	22.9
30,000-39,999	144	15.4
40,000-49,999	111	11.9
50,000-59,999	63	6.7
60,000-more	118	12.7
	933	100.0

Appendix E (continued)

Living Arrangements	Number	Percent
Living alone	207	22.1
Live with spouse only	552	59.0
Live with spouse & others	94	10.0
Live with others, not spouse	84	8.9
	937	100.0

Geographic Location	Number	Percent
East	157	17.0
North Central	350	37.6
South	263	28.3
West	159	17.1
	929	100.0

Employment Status	Number	Percent
Working	370	39.4
Not working	570	60.6
	940	100.0

Residence Location	Number	Percent
Urban	756	78.3
Rural	193	20.0
Don't know/not sure	16	1.7
	965	100.0

Appendix F
Need-Based Segments

A set of clusters was based on *consumption-related needs*. Measures of consumption-related needs were factor analyzed, and all the items with a factor loading of approximately .40 or higher were retained for further consideration. Table F.1 shows the factor analysis solution, factors extracted, and respective loadings. The four extracted factors were named based on their common meaning of the needs comprising each. Thus, Factor 1 was named "Activities of Daily Living" (ADLs), since the concern for the items on this factor deals with day-to-day tasks. Factor 2 was named "Selective Information," since needs for activities arise only on certain occasions, and decisions are relatively important. Factor 3 consisted of two items that suggested concern for "Security/Safety," while the last factor suggested a construct consisting of items of an "Economic" nature.

Factor scores from this solution were used as input into a cluster analysis program using Ward's method. Stress coefficients suggested four clusters, which were named after examining mean scores by cluster (Table F.2). The first cluster (N=374) was named "Self-Sufficients," the second (N=185) "Young Insecureds," the third (N=268) "Dependent Frail," and the last (N=123) "Struggling Full-nesters." Cross classification of selected responses were obtained by type of cluster for profiling these clusters.

Table F.1

Significant Factor Loadings Based on Factor Analysis of Consumption-Related Needs of Older Adults

	ADLs	Selective Information	Security/ Safety	Economic
Finding someone to do home or appliance repairs..		.62		
Getting good financial, tax or legal advice...		.80		
Being mugged, raped or robbed..			.88	
Having your home/apartment burned or burglarized..			.80	
Getting useful information on things that affect you...		.61		
Keeping your job or going back to work...				.71
Being able to do your shopping and run errands..	.84			
Being able to fix your meals..	.84			
Being able to attend special events or activities...	.77			
Being able to contact someone in case of emergency...	.68			
Being able to keep up with bills and weekly expenses...	.62			.39
Being financially independent...	.53			.39
Finding ways to enjoy yourself (like travel and entertainment)..	.54	.40		
Knowing where to call for assistance on what to do or how to do certain things...................................	.52	.46		
Losing your money (cash, checks or savings)...	.54			
Feeling that no one cares for you.....................................	.52			
Having to take care of your aging parents....................				.75
Factor	1	2	3	4

Table F.2
Cluster Means of Need Factors and Cluster Sizes

Cluster	Factor 1	Factor 2	Factor 3	Factor 4	N
1	-.55	.50	.31	-.44	373
2	-.07	-.39	.51	1.36	185
3	.65	-.69	-.19	-.60	268
4	.34	-1.30	-1.30	.59	123

Appendix G
Methodological Note

The following tables are provided for the reader who is interested in obtaining a quick estimate either of the stability of a given percentage or of the significance of the difference between two percentages.

Confidence Intervals for a Given Percentage
(at the 95% confidence level)

N		Reported Percentage			
	10 or	20 or	30 or	40 or	
Based for %	90%	80%	70%	60%	50%
1000	1.9	2.6	2.9	3.1	3.2
500	2.6	3.5	4.0	4.3	4.4
250	3.7	5.0	5.7	6.1	6.2
200	4.2	5.5	6.3	6.8	6.9
150	4.8	6.4	7.3	7.8	8.0
100	5.9	7.8	9.0	9.6	9.8
50	8.3	11.1	12.7	11.6	13.9
25	11.8	15.7	18.0	19.2	19.6

Example: If a report shows that 20% of all respondents (when N = 500) answer in a particular way, the chances are about 95 out of 100 that the true value is 20% + 3.5%, that is the range 23.5% - 16.5% contains the true value.

Significance of Differences Between Percentages
(95% confidence level)

Average of Reported Percentages

Average of the bases of Percentages Being Compared	10 or 90%	20 or 80%	30 or 70%	40 or 60%	50%
1000	2.7	3.6	4.1	4.4	4.5
500	3.7	4.9	5.7	6.1	6.2
250	5.2	7.1	8.1	8.6	8.8
200	5.9	7.8	8.9	9.6	9.8
150	6.8	9.1	10.3	11.0	11.3
100	8.3	11.0	12.7	13.6	13.9
50	11.7	15.7	18.0	19.2	19.7
25	16.7	22.2	25.5	27.2	27.7

Example: The data show that 33% of all respondents from 55 to 64 years of age use a certain service and that only 27% of all respondents in the 65 and over age group use that service. Could this difference be due to a chance?

Appendix G (continued)

In this example assume an average base of 500 for the represented percentages. The average of the percentages (33 + 27) equals 30% and the difference between the percentages is 6%.

Since 6% is greater than 5.7 (the figure in the table for this base and percentage) the chances are about 95 out of 100 that the service is used more by the 54-64 age group.

The table values are based on an assumption of simple random sampling. The figures may be too large if a stratified sampling technique was used and probably are too small if a cluster sampling technique was utilized. The second table should be used with extreme caution if the bases being averaged are very different.

References

American Association of Retired Persons (AARP) (1986). *Understanding Senior Housing—An AARP Survey of Consumers' Preferences, Concerns, and Needs.* Washington, DC: AARP Program Department.

——— (1990a). *Older Consumer Behavior.* Washington, DC: AARP.

——— (1990b). *Profile of Older Americans.* Washington, DC: AARP.

American Demographics (1988). "Shopper's Paradise" (May): 28.

——— (1990). "Demomemo" (July): 6.

——— (1991). "Private Labels Preferred" (February): 56.

American Society on Aging (1987). *Education in Aging for Scientists and Engineers.* San Francisco: American Society on Aging.

Atchley, Robert C. (1987). *Aging, Continuity and Change* (2nd ed.). Belmont, CA: Wadsworth Publishing Company.

Balkite, Richard (1988). "Maximizing Communications with Seniors Through Advertising, Public Relations and the 'Aging Network.' " Speech presented at the American Business and Aging Conference of the American Society on Aging. Washington, DC, September 29 and 30.

Barrow, George M., and Patricia A. Smith (1983). *Aging, the Individual and Society.* St. Paul, MN: West Publishing Company.

Bauer, D., and B. Warner (1978). "Where Did All the Jobs Go?" *Perspective on Aging* 7(1, January/February): 35–37.

Bernhardt, Kenneth L., and Thomas C. Kinnear (1976). "Profiling the Senior Citizen Market." *Advances in Consumer Research* 3: 449–452.

Bernstein, Peter (1978). "Psychographics Still an Issue on Madison Avenue." *Fortune* (January 16): 78–84.

Burton, John R., and Charles B. Hennon (1980). "Consumer Concerns of Senior Citizen Center Participants." *Journal of Consumer Affairs* 14(2, Winter); 366–382.

Dibner, Andrew S., Louis Lowy, and John Morris (1982). "Usage and Acceptance of an Emergency Alarm System by the Frail Elderly." *Gerontologist* 22(December): 538.

Doolittle, J. C. (1979). "News Media Use by Older Adults." *Journalism Quarterly* 56(2): 311–317, 345.

Dychtwald, Ken, and Joe Flower (1989). *Age Wave*. Los Angeles: Jeremy P. Tarcher, Inc.

Exter, Thomas (1986). "Looking for Brand Loyalty." *American Demographics* (April): 32–33, 52–56.

Fishbein, Gershon (1975). "Congregate Housing—With a Difference." *Geriatrics* 30(9): 124–128.

Fox, J. A. (1980). "Consumer Protection and the Elderly." In Resource Network, *The Elderly Consumer*. Rosslyn, VA: Consumer Education Resource Network.

French, W., et al. (1983). "The Problem of Older Consumers: Comparison of England, Israel, Norway and the United States." In *Proceedings of the American Marketing Association Conference*, 390–395. Chicago: American Marketing Association.

Gatignon, Hubert, and Thomas S. Robertson (1985). "A Propositional Inventory for New Diffusion Research." *Journal of Consumer Research* 11(4, March): 849–867.

Gelb, Betsy D. (1978). "Exploring the Gray Market Segment." *MSU Business Topics* 26(Spring): 41–46.

——— (1982). "Discovering the 65+ Consumer." *Business Horizons* 25(3, May/June): 42–46.

Gibler, Karen Martin (1990). "Economic Life-Cycle Hypothesis and Home Equity Dissaving Behavior." Unpublished Ph.D. dissertation. Atlanta: Georgia State University.

Gillett, Peter L., and Robert L. Schneider (1978). "Community-wide Discount Programs for Older Persons: A Review and Evaluation." *Journal of Consumer Affairs* 12(2, Winter): 309–322.

Gilly, Mary C., and Valarie A. Zeithaml (1985). "The Elderly Consumer and Adoption of Technologies." *Journal of Consumer Research* 12(December): 353–357.

Goldring & Company (1987). *Geromarket Study*. Chicago: Goldring & Company.

Gollub, James, and Harold Javitz (1989). "Six Ways to Age." *American Demographics* 11(June): 28, 30, 35, 56–57.

Greco, Alan J. (1988). "The Elderly as Communicators: Perceptions of Advertising Practitioners." *Journal of Advertising Research* (June-July): 39–46.

Greco, Alan, and Linda E. Swayne (1992). "Sales Responses of Elderly Consumers to Point-of-Purchase Advertising." *Journal of Advertising Research* (September/October):43–53.

Gross, A. (1989). "Tapping the Golden Years." *Adweek's Marketing Week Supplement* (November 6): 16–17.

Hoy, Mariea Grubbs, and Raymond P. Fisk (1985). "Older Consumers and Services: Implications for Marketers." In *AMA Educators Proceedings*, edited by Robert F. Lusch et al., 51–55. Chicago: American Marketing Association.

Ingrassia, Paul, and Gregory A. Patterson (1989), "Is Buying a Car a Choice or a Chore?" *The Wall Street Journal* (October 24): B1, B6.

Jordan, Case, and McGrath, Inc. (1983). *The 55+ Market: The Marketing Opportunity of the 1980s*. New York: Jordan, Case and McGrath, Inc.

Kahana, Eva, and J. Felton (1977). "Social Context and Personal Need: A Study of Polish and Jewish Aged." *Journal of Social Issues*, 33(4).

Kerschner, Paul A., and Kathleen A. Chelsving (1981). "The Aged User and Technology." Paper presented at the Conference on Communications Technology and the Elderly: Issues and Forecasts. Cleveland, OH, October 22–23.

Kotler, Philip (1984). *Marketing Management* (5th ed.) Englewood Cliffs, NJ: Prentice-Hall.

Kubey, Robert W. (1980). "Television and Aging: Past, Present and Future." *The Gerontologist* 20 (February): 16–35.

Lambert, Zarrel V., Paul L. Doering, Eric Goldstein, and William C. McCormick (1980). "Predisposition Toward Generic Drug Acceptance." *Journal of Consumer Research* 7(June): 14–23.

Lazer, William (1985). "Inside the Mature Market." *American Demographics* (March): 23–25, 48–49.

——— (1986). "Dimensions of the Mature Market." *Journal of Consumer Marketing* 3(3): 23–33.

——— (1987). *Handbook of Demographics for Marketing and Advertising: Sources and Trends on the U.S. Consumer.* Lexington, MA: Lexington Books.

Lazer, William, and Eric H. Shaw (1987). "How Older Americans Spend Their Money." *American Demographics* 19(9, September): 36–41.

Lee, Gary R. (1983). "Social Integration and Fear of Crime among Older Persons." *Journal of Gerontology* 38(6); 745–750.

Little, Virginia C. (1980). "Assessing the Needs of the Elderly: State of the Art." *International Journal of Aging and Human Development*, 11(1): 65–76.

Lumpkin, James R., Marjorie J. Caballero, and Lawrence B. Chonko (1987). *Direct Marketing to the Elderly: Sources of Dissatisfaction and Remedies.* Final report to the AARP Andrus Foundation. Waco, TX: Baylor University, June.

Lumpkin, James R., and Barnett A. Greenberg (1982). "Apparel Shopping Patterns of the Elderly Consumers." *Journal of Retailing* 58(4, Winter): 68–89.

Lumpkin, James R., Barnett A. Greenberg, and Jac L. Goldstucker (1985). "Marketplace Needs of the Elderly: Determinant Attributes and Store Choice." *Journal of Retailing* 61(2, Summer): 75–105.

Marketing News (1987). "Over-50 Group Skeptical of Efforts to Change Shopping Patterns" (May 22): 27.

Markle Foundation (1988). *Pioneers on the Frontier of Life: Aging in America (Summary Report).* New York: The Markle Foundation.

Mason, J. Barry, and William O. Bearden (1978). "Profiling the Shopping Behavior of Elderly Consumers." *The Gerontologist* 18(October): 454–461.

——— (1980). "Attitudes Toward and Use of Alternative Credit Sources by Elderly Consumers." *The Journal of Consumer Credit Management* 12(1, Summer): 2–9.

Mathur, Anil, and George P. Moschis (1992). "Use of Credit by Older Americans." Paper presented at the Conference of the American Marketing Association. Chicago, August.

Maturity Market Perspectives (1990). "Bank Programs Still Missing 55 to 64 Group" (September): 1.

——— (1992). "Senior Discounts May Be Discontinued." (March 1): 2.

Maturity Market Report (1988). "New Research on Healthcare Decision Makers." 2(4, April): 6–7.

Maurer, Richard C., James A. Christenson, and Paul D. Warner (1980). "Perspectives of Community Services Among Rural and Urban Elderly." Paper presented at the Rural Sociological Society Conference.

McMillan, Pat, and George P. Moschis (1985). *The Silver Wave: A Look at the 55+ Market.* Atlanta: BellSouth Corporation, Market Research and Strategy Division.

Meddis, Sam, and Jeanne DeQuine (1987). "The Young, Not Elderly, Are Most Often Victims of Crime." *USA Today* (November 23): 3A.

Michman, R., R. Hocking, and L. Harris (1981). "Are Senior Citizens Responsive to New Cold Product Promotions?" In *Progress in Marketing Theory and Practice,* edited by R. Taylor, J. Summey, and B. Bergiel, 102–104. Carbondale, IL: Southern Marketing Association.

Miklos, Pam (1982). *The Supermarket Shopper Experience of the Older Consumers: A Qualitative Research Report.* Washington, DC: Food Marketing Institute.

Milliman, Ronald E., and Robert C. Erffmeyer (1990). "Improving Advertising Aimed at Seniors." *Journal of Advertising Research* (December/January): 31–36.

Money (1987). *Americans and Their Money 5,* the Fifth National Survey. New York: Time Inc. Magazine Co.

Moschis, George P. (1987). *Consumer Socialization: A Life Cycle Perspective.* Lexington, MA: Lexington Books.

——— (1989). *Older Consumer Responses to Marketing Activities of Select Industry Groups.* Atlanta: Georgia State University, Center for Mature Consumer Studies.

——— (1990). "Frameworks for Studying Older Consumers: Present Status and Methodological Issues." Working paper. Atlanta: Georgia State University, Center for Mature Consumer Studies.

——— (1992a). "Gerontographics." *Journal of Services Marketing* 6(3, Summer): 17–26.

——— (1992b). *Marketing to Older Consumers.* Westport, CT: Quorum.

Moschis, George P., and Barbara B. Payne (1991). *Explanations of the Low Food Stamp Utilization Rates among Low-Income Elderly: Sociological and Psychological Perspectives.* Washington, DC: U.S. Department of Agriculture, Food and Nutrition Service.

Moschis, George P., et al. (1991). *Intergenerational Consumer Perceptions: Changing Needs in a Changing Society.* Atlanta: Georgia State University, Center for Mature Consumer Studies.

Murrel, Stanley A., James M. Brockway, and Paul Schulte (1982). "The Kentucky Elderly Need Assessment: Concurrent Validity of Different Measures of Unmet Needs." *American Journal of Community Psychology* 10(2): 117–132.

Nasar, Jack L., and Mitra Farokhpay (1985). "Assessment of Activity Priorities and Design Preferences of Elderly Residents in Public Housing: A Case Study." *Gerontologist* 25(3, June): 251–257.

National Food Processors Association (1990). *Food Labeling and Nutrition: What Americans Want.* Washington, DC: National Food Processors Association.

Neugarten, Bernice (1977). "Personality and Aging." In *Handbook in Psychology of Aging*, 2d ed., edited by James E. Birren and K. Warner Schaie, 626–649. New York: Van Nostrand Reinhold Company.

Noeske, Nancy R. (1987). "Communicating with the Elder Consumer." Paper presented at the American Society Conference on Business and Aging. Washington, DC, September 30.

Norton, Lee, and Michael Courlander (1982). "Fear of Crime among the Elderly: The Role of Crime Prevention Programs." *The Gerontologist* 22(4): 388.

Novak, Thomas P., and Bruce MacEvoy (1990). "On Comparing Alternative Segmentation Schemes: The List of Values (LOV) and Values and Lifestyles (VALS)." *Journal of Consumer Research* 7(June): 105–109.

O'Driscoll, Patrick (1987). "Aging Picture not as Gray as We Paint It." *USA Today* (May 18): 1A–2A.

Osborn, A. F. (1963). *Applied Imagination*, 3rd ed. New York: Charles Scribner & Sons.

Payment Systems, Inc. (1982). *Payment Systems Perspectives '82*. Atlanta: Payment Systems, Inc.

"Personality and Consumer Behavior: An Update." (1991). In *Perspectives in Consumer Behavior*, edited by Harold H. Kassarjian and Thomas S. Robertson, 281–316. Englewood Cliffs, NJ: Prentice-Hall.

Pieper, Alicia U. (1968). *Survey of Clothing Needs of Women 65 and Older*. Stark County, OH: Kent State University.

Prisuta, Richard, and Robert Kriner (1985). "Communications Technology and Older Persons." Paper presented at the International Communication Association Conference. Honolulu, HI, May 23–28.

Reiner, Thomas A. (1990). *Expenditure Patterns of the Elderly*. Prepared for the Andrus Foundation. Washington, DC: AARP Andrus Foundation.

Schewe, Charles (1984). "Buying and Consuming Behavior of the Elderly: Findings from Behavioral Research." *Advances in Consumer Research* (11): 558–562.

——— (1985). "Gray America Goes to Market." *Business* 35(April- June): 3–9.

Schutz, Howard G., Pamela C. Baird, and Glenn R. Hawkes (1979). *Lifestyles and Consumer Behavior of Older Americans*. New York: Praeger.

Selling to Seniors (1989). "Companies Are Missing the Mark in Trying to Reach Middle-to-Upper Income Seniors." Silver Spring, MD: CD Publications, May 10.

Senior Market Report (1988). "Of Consuming Interest to Domestic Manufacturers" 1(11, November): 4.

Sharkey, Betsy (1988). "Looking at the Elderly-to-Be." *Adweek*, Special Report (November 21): 29–30.

Sherman, E., and M. Brittain (1973). "Contemporary Food Gatherers: A Study of Food Shopping Habits of an Elderly Urban Population." *The Gerontologist* 1(13): 358–364.

Sirgy, Joseph M. (1982). "Self-Concept in Consumer Behavior: A Critical Review." *Journal of Consumer Research* 9(December): 287–300.

——— (1986). *Self-Congruity: Toward a Theory of Personality and Cybernetics*. New York: Praeger.

Smith, Kelly, Anil Mathur, and George P. Moschis (1990). "The Elderly's Motivations for Gift-Giving: An Exchange Theory Perspective." In *AMA Ed-*

ucators' Conference Proceedings, 82–87. Chicago: American Marketing Association.

Smith, Ruth B., and George P. Moschis (1985). "A Socialization Perspective on Selected Consumer Characteristics of the Elderly." *Journal of Consumer Affairs* 19(1, Spring/Summer): 74–95.

Sofranko, Andrew J., Frederic C. Fliegel, and Nina Glasgow (1982–1983). "Older Urban Migrants in Rural Settings: Problems and Prospects." *International Aging and Human Development* 16(4): 297–309.

Stanley, Thomas J., Murphy A. Sewall, and George P. Moschis (1982). *Profiling Consumers by Payment Methods*. Atlanta: Payment Systems, Inc.

Swartz, Teresa A., and Nancy Stephens (1984). "Information Search for Services: The Maturity Segment." In *Advances in Consumer Research*, vol. 11, edited by T. Kinnear, 244–249. Provo, UT: Association for Consumer Research.

Uncles, Mark D., and Andrew S. C. Ehrenberg (1990). "Brand Choice among Older Consumers." *Journal of Advertising Research* 30(August/September): 19–22.

USA Today (1985). "Older People Have the Most." (October 24): 4B.

U.S. Bureau of Labor Statistics (1989). *Consumer Expenditure Survey*. Washington, DC: U.S. Bureau of Labor Statistics.

U.S. Bureau of the Census (1990). *Household Wealth and Asset Ownership, 1988*. Current Population Reports, Series P–70, No. 22. Washington, DC: U.S. Government Printing Office.

Tongren, H. N. (1988). "Determinant Behavior Characteristics of Older Consumers." *Journal of Consumer Affairs* 22(1): 136–137.

Towle, Jeffry G., and Claude R. Martin (1976). "The Elderly Consumer: One Segment or Many?" *Advances in Consumer Research* (3): 463–468.

VanDellen, Robert J. (1990). *Healthcare Advertising: Consumer Responses and Attitudes*. Cadillac, MI: Healthcare Marketing and Communication, Inc.

VanGundy, Arthur B. (1983). "Brainwriting for New Product Ideas." *Journal of Consumer Marketing* 1(2, Fall): 67–74.

Ward, Bernice (1989). "Marketers Slow to Catch Age Wave." *Advertising Age* (May 22): S1–S8.

Whirlpool Corporation (1983). *America's Search for Quality*. Benton Harbor, MI: Whirlpool Corporation.

Yankelovich, Daniel (1987). *The Mature Americans*. New York: Daniel Yankelovich Group, Inc.

Zbytniewski, Jo-Ann (1979). "The Older Shopper: Over 65 and Overlooked?" *Progressive Grocer* (November): 109–111.

Ziff, Ruth (1984). "Characteristics of the Market: Demographics and Attitudes." Paper presented to the Center on Aging. Hershey, PA, May 8.

Index

About the Author

GEORGE P. MOSCHIS is Professor of Marketing and the founder and director of the Center for Mature Consumer Studies at Georgia State University, where he is also a member of the Gerontology Program Faculty. A pioneer in developing educational materials on marketing to older adults, Dr. Moschis received the 1990 SAGE award for his exemplary work in this field, and his center was recognized by *American Demographics* magazine for four consecutive years as one of the best sources of marketing information. He is a frequent speaker at business forums, and author of *Marketing to Older Consumers* (Quorum, 1992) and *Consumer Socialization: A Life-Cycle Perspective* (1987).